W9-DIO-813

Jacob Piatt Dunn, Jr.:
A Life in History and Politics,
1855–1924

To Dad:
   The best father a son
could ever hope to have.
Thanks for always being
there when I needed you
and for your devotion all
these years. You're a big
part of this book. I hope
you enjoy it,

                Love,
                   your son,

Jacob Piatt Dunn, Jr.:
A Life in History and Politics, 1855–1924

Ray E. Boomhower

INDIANA HISTORICAL SOCIETY
INDIANAPOLIS 1997

The paper in this publication meets the minimum requirements of
American National Standard for Information Sciences—Permanence
of Paper for Printed Library Materials, ANSI Z39.48-1984. ∞

Library of Congress Cataloging-in-Publication Data

Boomhower, Ray E., 1959-
    Jacob Piatt Dunn, Jr. : a life in history and politics, 1855–1924
    / Ray E. Boomhower.
       p.   cm.
    Includes bibliographical references and index.
    ISBN 0-87195-119-3
    1. Dunn, Jacob Piatt, 1855–1924. 2. Historians--Indiana--
Biography. 3. Politicians--Indiana--Biography. 4. Journalists--
Indiana--Biography. 5. Indiana--Politics and government.
    I. Title.
    F526.B73   1997
    977.2'041092--dc21
    [B]   97-23545
                                                CIP

For Megan L. McKee

Who in so many ways made this work possible.

"You have to make more noise than anybody else, you have to make yourself more obtrusive than anybody else, you have to fill all the papers more than anybody else, in fact you have to be there all the time and see that they do not snow you under, if you are really going to get your reform realized."

Emmeline Pankhurst, English suffragist, 1913

Contents

Preface

IN AN ARTICLE FOR *HARPER'S MAGAZINE* BARBARA TUCHMAN, author of such best-selling books as *The Proud Tower*, *The Guns of August*, and *The March to Folly*, contemplated the question of the meaning of her work, a query she was not at all happy to ponder. "No one," she complained, "asks the novelist why he writes novels or the poet what is his purpose in writing poems." The same criteria, Tuchman said, should be used for writing, studying, and reading history, which ought to be done for its own sake. "Insistence on a purpose turns the historian into a prophet—and that is another profession," she added.[1]

Frankly, Tuchman's comments make sense to one who has been asked countless times, sometimes by the same person over and over again, "Why a biography of Jacob Piatt Dunn, Jr.? What did he do to deserve such an effort?" I always yearned to respond in these situations with a glib, "Why not?," but instead I decided to provide a serious answer: "It was all a mistake." I had never intended to take as much time as I have in pursuing the life and times of Mr. Dunn, a journey my wife Megan has jokingly (I think) called "an obsession."

It all started back in 1992 when I had to come up with an original idea for a paper for my seminar class in United States history at Indiana University-Purdue University at Indianapolis. Luckily, I had just written a "Destination Indiana" column for the Indiana Historical Society's illustrated history magazine, *Traces of Indiana and Midwestern*

History, on the career of Hoosier vice president Thomas R. Marshall, whose wit enlivened the two administrations of President Woodrow Wilson. As Indiana governor from 1909 to 1913, Marshall, often described as a "Progressive with the brakes on," did manage to enact a number of reform measures. In one instance, however, an attempt to revise the state's constitution, he met with defeat. I thought, and my professor agreed, that this battle over the Indiana constitution would make the perfect subject for my paper.

In doing my research I was shocked to discover that the real credit for this unique method at constitutional reform should not go to Marshall, but to another man, the aforementioned Dunn. It soon became clear to me that in Indiana, in the late nineteenth and early twentieth centuries, no one had a greater impact on the political life of Hoosiers, particularly on the issue of suffrage, than Jacob Piatt Dunn, Jr. As an amateur historian who became immersed in the cauldron of political activity that marked Indiana's history as a pivotal state in national politics, Dunn left behind riveting firsthand accounts of those heady days and the reform efforts he and others undertook to save the state's tarnished reputation. The full story of Dunn's influence on the political activities he described in such multivolume works as *Indiana and Indianans* and *Greater Indianapolis*, both of which remain standard works today, has rarely been scrutinized, a situation I hope is rectified through the following pages. Dunn should also be remembered for his unstinting efforts to save the nineteenth state's heritage, especially his revitalization of the Indiana Historical Society and the Indiana State Library, and his painstaking attempts to preserve the language of the Miami Indians.

Many people have had a hand in helping prepare this book for publication. For their comments on an earlier version of this work, which was eventually published in the December 1994 issue of the *Indiana Magazine of History* as "'To Secure Honest Elections': Jacob Piatt Dunn, Jr., and the Reform of Indiana's Ballot," I am indebted to Dr. Robert G. Barrows, Indiana University-Purdue University at Indianapolis associate professor of history; Dr. James H. Madison, Indiana University History Department chairman; and Lorna Lutes Sylvester, *Indiana Magazine of History* associate editor. Members of my thesis committee, Dr. Ralph Gray and Dr. Scott Seregny, also provided thoughtful and helpful suggestions for improvements.

Also providing invaluable assistance and advice on this and the earlier work have been the following Indiana Historical Society staff: my wife, Megan McKee, editor; J. Kent Calder, *Traces of Indiana and Midwestern History* managing editor; Paula Corpuz, senior editor; Shirley McCord, editor; and Thomas Mason, Publications Division director. Thanks also to Kathy Breen, assistant editor, who painstakingly checked every footnote for accuracy.

I would also like to thank the staffs at the Indiana Historical Society's William Henry Smith Memorial Library, the Indiana State Archives, the Lilly Library at Indiana University, and the Indiana State Library's Indiana Division for their assistance in securing the documents, photographs, and materials needed for researching and publishing this book. I would like to offer particular thanks to the staff of the State Library's Newspaper Section for its support. Tom Hamm at Earlham College provided essential information on Dunn's days as a student at that Quaker institution. Stewart Rafert of the University of Delaware provided helpful comments on Dunn's work with the Miami Indian language.

Of course, all the errors and misunderstandings in the book are mine and mine alone.

Introduction

FREDERICK M. DAVENPORT, A STAFF CORRESPONDENT FOR THE
weekly New York City newspaper *The Outlook*, traveled
extensively throughout the Middle West in the spring of
1916 gathering information on the upcoming presidential
nomination campaign. One of the places he visited was Indiana, which at the time had often played a pivotal role in
national elections. Reflecting on the Hoosier State, Davenport wrote that back East, Indiana had the "reputation politically of being sodden, mediocre, deeply satisfied with
things as they are provided they are bad enough." He char-
acterized the state's party managers as "flat, insipid, and
platitudinous." The reporter went on to portray Indiana as
the "original lair of the stand-patter in the United States."[1]

Davenport's assessment of the nineteenth state had more
than a little basis in fact. During the late nineteenth and
early twentieth centuries, Indiana, as Democratic United
States senator Daniel W. Voorhees termed it, was the "Bel-
gium of politics, the debatable land between great contending parties and opinions."[2] Democrats and Republicans battled fiercely to sway Indiana voters to their cause by such
means as naming Hoosiers to their national tickets, usually
as vice president. From 1840 to 1940 almost 60 percent of
the national elections had Indiana politicians on the ballot.
One Republican official in 1876 went as far as to claim that
"a bloody shirt campaign, with money, and Indiana is safe;
a financial campaign and no money and we are beaten." As
an "October state" from 1851 through 1880, with elections

for state and local officials held a month before the regular election, Indiana offered to political parties a sounding board on the mood of the voters. The state's prominence in national politics, however, came with a price. Party managers used whatever means necessary to garner votes for their candidates, including importing voters from out of state and outright vote buying. Such activities won for Indiana, noted a historian of the period, an "unenviable reputation for political corruption."[3]

Corruption had become so commonplace in the Hoosier State that those working at the grassroots level for their party of choice offered as proof of their loyalty the fact that they had "risked the penitentiary" on its behalf. Fellowships formed across party lines as workers on either side held little or no fear of harsh penalties being enacted if they were caught dealing in some shady political maneuvering. "Usually after a warm campaign there were several arrests, and sometimes indictments, but there was always an 'exchange of prisoners.'"[4]

Disgusted with the political situation in his state, Republican attorney William P. Fishback, in a plea for honest elections before students of the state university in 1886, offered the following assessment:

If Nathaniel Hawthorne's magic bugle were to summon into line— clothed in proper raiment of horizontal stripes, all the rascals who bribed voters, or who took bribes for their votes, who corrupted election officers, or falsified election returns, who swore in illegal votes, who colonized voters, who voted twice, or voted double tickets, who tampered with ballots after they were cast, who consorted with or encouraged repeaters and ballot-box stuffers, or who were accessory to their escape from the just penalties of the violated law, it would be, I fear, a large procession, in which we should see both parties represented, and in which we might discover men of good repute, as the phrase goes, and some who have had and now have official preferment mainly because they had earned a place in that procession.[5]

Deploring the sorry situation of Hoosier politics—he claimed that the state, because of its pivotal status, had been reduced to a "pitiable condition of political corruption

Indiana State Library

Front cover of *Frank Leslie's Illustrated Weekly Newspaper* for the week ending 17 November 1888, picturing the celebration outside Benjamin Harrison's Indianapolis home upon his election as president

. . . and both the great parties had been exhausting the resources of political depravity to carry it"[6]—one man, Jacob Piatt Dunn, Jr., an attorney, journalist, Indiana historian, and Democrat, was in the vanguard of a reform endeavor stretching from the late nineteenth to the early twentieth century and dedicated to cleansing the sordid reputation Indiana had earned for itself through election chicanery. From

Jacob Piatt Dunn, Jr.

his key role in adopting the Australian ballot system in Indiana to his ultimately failed attempt at enacting a new
state constitution, Dunn, working both behind the scenes

and in public, did more than anyone, including elected officials, to reduce fraud and ensure honest elections in Indiana. To Dunn, securing honesty in elections was *the* key issue facing the country during his lifetime. "The corruption
of the ballot," he argued, "destroys the very foundation of
popular government, and if that be not guarded, the rest is
not worth guarding."[7]

Through his work on electoral and other reforms—shep-
herding through a new city charter for Indianapolis, establishing free public libraries throughout the state, and revi-
talizing such historical institutions as the Indiana
Historical Society and the Indiana State Library—and his
historical writing, Dunn hoped to reverse Indiana's poor national reputation and to inspire Hoosiers to take a genuine
sense of pride in their state. Although Dunn mainly blamed
Indiana's political corruption for its sordid national standing, the historian pointed out that part of the blame also
rested on "ignorance on the part of ourselves and of the
world at large of what Indiana has to be proud of. . . . We
put in our time reading Eastern periodicals, studying European politics, and striving in general to keep up with what
we call the progress of the century, instead of noting the real
progress that is being made on all sides of us."[8]

Dunn's reform efforts came during an era when politicians, journalists, writers, lawyers, labor leaders, and others on the local, state, and national levels were attempting
to rectify what they believed were iniquities in American
life. This diverse group by no means agreed upon what reforms were needed. Some wanted to prohibit the consump-
tion of alcohol, others hoped to lessen the powerful hold
business trusts had on the country, and still others fought
for women's suffrage. Drawing together these disparate
aims was a shared sense of what one scholar of the period
termed "optimism, morality, and activism."[9] They also
shared such values as a faith in majority government; the
firm belief that people should control their government,
both before and after elections; and a conviction that citizens had an obligation to participate in forming their government.[10]

Again and again, however, Dunn came back to the point
that the greatest obstacle standing in the way of good government was the corruption of voters. "Of what possible
benefit is it to have direct primaries, if the candidate can
purchase his nomination?" he asked. "Of what avail the initiative, referendum, or recall if your appeal is to a de-
bauched electorate? What adds whether women vote or not,
if enough voters are controlled to fix the result of the election?" In reality, Dunn proclaimed, without honest elections
it would be "impossible" to have popular government. His
fondest wish would be the power to "sound in the ear of every voter in the country the solemn warning that if we do
not eradicate the corruption of the suffrage in this country
it will ruin our government."[11] Improving the quality of the
Hoosier voter took the form almost of a crusade for Dunn.
He did everything in his power to cleanse the state's ballot,
even disfranchising those who he believed failed to meet his
stringent qualifications for suffrage.

For one who often railed against the depravity of party
regulars, both Democrat and Republican alike, Dunn preferred to engage in his reform activities from within a party
structure, in his case the Democratic party, essentially becoming a partisan reformer—one whose reform endeavors
tended, at least in Dunn's mind, to benefit the Democratic
party. In his strong identification with a political organization, Dunn typified others who came of age politically in the
late nineteenth century, the Gilded Age, a time when parties "dominated government more thoroughly than they
ever had before or would again."[12] Partisanship particularly
ran deep in the Midwest. In both cities and on the farm, the
vast majority of people in the region, at least 90 percent, allied themselves with either the Republican or Democratic
party.[13]

Dunn merged his political, reform, and historical interests throughout his career. His daughter, Caroline Dunn,
who followed in her father's footsteps by pursuing a career
in a number of Indiana libraries, noted that her father was
fascinated with politics. Much of his writing, she said, was
"political or politico-economical."[14] In an article titled "Duty

of the State to Its History," which appeared in the December 1910 issue of the *Indiana Magazine of History*, Dunn set out his philosophy about the blending of history and politics. He agreed with the Roman historian Tacitus that the "chief use of history is to promote good government." Dunn noted that the democracy of his own day was a far cry from the absolute monarchy of Tacitus's time. He theorized:

> History in our times is the record of progress in civilization and government. It is the record of the experience of the state, and a state should profit by its experience just as an individual does. But there is this difference: An individual carries the memory of his experience with him, while the governing powers of a state are frequently changed, and the experience of one generation is lost to following ones, unless it be recorded in some permanent way.[15]

Dunn warned government officials that their actions in office—both good and bad—would be recorded for posterity. He also stressed the importance for future generations to know about the past "in order to hand down the goodly heritage of civilization and government that comes to their hands."[16] Also, as a historian, Dunn believed that he had an obligation to keep watch over "history in the making, and point out evils to be avoided." Throughout his career he made a habit of pointing out those "evils to be avoided," often engaging in spirited debates in Indianapolis newspapers with those who drew his wrath, and offered suggestions for ways to lessen their effect on the body politic.[17]

During his opening speech in his 1902 campaign for Congress in Indiana's Seventh Congressional District, Dunn expounded on his political beliefs for Hoosier voters. He declared that he believed fully in what he called the "American theory of government," with nations having the right to decide their own fate without interference from outside governments. This had to be true, he said, because "any people must know their own needs better than any other people know them, and they are more interested in getting good government for themselves than any other people can be in giving them good government." Although people are often guided more by prejudice, desire for gain, or "unfounded hopes and fears" than by reason, Dunn expressed the belief

Hoosiers parade for support of GOP presidential candidate William McKinley in Delphi, Indiana, during the 1896 election

that the "great majority of the people really want what is right."[18]

The Hoosier historian stood by his convictions in practice as well as in theory by becoming actively involved in the reform issues cited above. Dunn knew that the successful passage of reform measures would not necessarily turn sinners into saints, but he believed such legislation could "prevent them from reaping the fruits of dishonesty." He reasoned that the best way to stop suspected evil was "to take away, as far as possible, the motive for wrong-doing." Once men understood that they could violate the law at will, Dunn warned that "you will have as many varieties of violation as you have men to deal with." The public, he said, first had to be convinced of the nature of the evil to be remedied. Once that had been accomplished, officials could then convince voters to utilize a "rational remedy." Dunn used a folksy example to illustrate his idea, noting that a doctor may know how to treat rheumatism but he could not make any progress if a patient "thinks he can cure it by carrying a buckeye in his pocket."[19]

Although Dunn's reforming zeal seemed to be in line with the Progressive Era's faith in having the right laws, en-

IHS, C7055

A political parade, complete with flag-draped horses, in Carroll County, Indiana, during the 1896 presidential campaign

forced by the right men, producing the right results, there was a difference.[20] He mixed his crusades for transformations of the Hoosier State with a healthy dose of Democratic party politics. Dunn reveled in the give-and-take of frontline politics and used his considerable writing skills on behalf of the Democrats. Although some of his Democratic friends considered him a mugwump—independent in his political beliefs—Dunn pointed out that all of his Republican associates "consider me a hide-bound Democrat; and I freely confess that I have a Democratic bias." He had this bias because he believed in "Democratic principles, and I know that they can be attained only through having Democrats in office."[21]

Although he fought for political reform throughout his life, Dunn could never be mistaken for those reformers dismissed by Tammany Hall leader George Washington Plunkitt as "mornin' glories—looked lovely in the mornin' and withered up in a short time."[22] Dunn had little respect during campaigns for Prohibitionists, Socialists, and Social Labor parties that were too busy engaging in a "noble fight for the vindication of their principles" actually to elect their candidates. The object of an election, he pointed out, is to "choose officers to conduct the government, and they never will catch it; so there is no occasion for wasting any time considering them."[23] Dunn remained loyal to the Democratic party even if it meant being forced out of his position as Indianapolis city controller by a Democratic mayor looking for a scapegoat for financial irregularities practiced by his political appointees. Of course, Dunn was not blind to the party's faults. Ruminating on the propensity of some Democratic politicians to immerse themselves in electoral fraud, even when they knew the party could never hope to compete with the GOP in obtaining funds for such activities, Dunn admitted that it was "too much to expect all Democrats to have common sense."[24]

The Hoosier historian's unwavering campaign for good government and honest elections, however, had another side. Like many of his Progressive Era contemporaries he distrusted the impact immigrants and African Americans might have on elections and devised measures to "restrict the franchise to the well-bred, 'deserving' citizens of the community."[25] If citizens wanted good government, Dunn claimed, suffrage must be available only to "those who can reasonably be supposed to feel some interest in good government."[26] The legislation Dunn authored to secure a virtuous suffrage restricted voting rights to those who could read and write. He asserted that suffrage had "debased the negro, on the average, instead of elevating him. . . . It has made him insolent and quarrelsome instead of self-respecting." Because he believed that the right to vote was based on the state's best interests, it would be unkind to give an African American "a right that is injuring him and injuring the State also." It would not be unjust, he continued, in denying voting rights "to the negro who remains illiterate, shiftless or criminal."[27]

And yet, the man who referred to his laundryman in Washington, D.C., during his time as secretary to Democratic Indiana senator Samuel M. Ralston, as a "Chink" and a guide he hired on a prospecting trip to Haiti as a "coon," also worked to preserve the cultural and linguistic history of Indiana's Miami Indians. According to Caroline Dunn, her father regarded a Native American as neither "'savage' nor 'noble,' but as another human being! He had a sympathetic attitude toward them and an understanding of their point of view in the treatment accorded them by the whites and by the United States government."[28] Dunn also displayed a more progressive attitude on the subject of women's rights. At the Indiana Historical Society's annual meeting on 27 December 1888, Dunn sponsored a resolution stating to the membership that it was "the sense of the Society that ladies were admissible to membership." His attempt to open the all-male Society membership to women failed, and it took until 1907 for the first female—Eliza Browning—to become a member.[29]

The seeming contradictions in Dunn's character—a belief in the power of the people to change their government, but one who wished to limit suffrage to a deserving few; a man who used racist language, but one who championed the cause of preserving Native Americans' languages—was a trait shared by other Progressives of the day and helps contribute to the difficulty in defining just what being a Progressive means. As Daniel T. Rodgers notes in his essay "In Search of Progressivism," Progressives could be found who both admired big corporations and hated trusts, who, like Dunn, "lauded the 'people' and who yearned for an electorate confined to white and educated voters, who spoke the language of social engineering and the language of moralistic uplift, or (to make matters worse) did all of these things at once."[30]

Whatever his prejudices, Dunn deserves the lion's share of credit for restoring honesty to Hoosier elections. His determined struggle throughout his life to ensure the purity of the ballot typified the historian's perspective on life. This was an outlook that could not be confined merely to recording the facts for posterity; Dunn was happiest as an active participant in the political process. He used his experiences in his various reform efforts—fighting for the Australian ballot law, securing a new city charter for Indianapolis, and drafting a new constitution for the state—to produce engrossing personal records of Indiana's history in such multivolume works as *Greater Indianapolis* (the standard history of Indianapolis for more than eighty years) and *Indiana and Indianans*. His fusion of history and politics, and his passion for reform, continue to affect Hoosiers' lives. Every time a voter goes into a voting booth, closes the curtain, pulls a lever, and makes a choice for representation in secrecy; every time a patron checks out a book at his local library; every time a researcher uses the materials at the Society and state library—all of these activities happen in large part because of Dunn and his lifelong commitment to the betterment of life in Indiana.

1

Early Life and Influences

IN THE EARLY SUMMER OF 1924 A REPORTER FOR THE *INDI-anapolis News*, preparing an obituary on the life and career of Jacob Piatt "Jake" Dunn, Jr., a leading citizen, asked for a comment from United States senator Samuel M. Ralston. The former Indiana governor had nothing but praise for the man who worked as his private secretary in Washington, D.C. Expressing his admiration for his deceased friend, Ralston noted that when the two had returned to Indianapolis from the nation's capital he could tell that something was wrong and that death was near. Characteristically, Ralston's friend and fellow Democrat was convinced he would be all right. "His will power was strong," Ralston said of Dunn, "and he was slow to admit that he could not accomplish anything he undertook. The idea of his having to surrender to the will of any man or even to physical troubles was to him apparently a preposterous thought."[1]

This stubbornness, even in the face of the illness that killed him, stood Dunn in good stead throughout his life as he battled to reform Indiana's wayward electoral system during the Progressive Era and struggled to save Indiana's history from being carelessly lost. It was a stubbornness he came by honestly from his father, a prospector, farmer, trader, and merchant, and which the junior Dunn shared with his eldest daughter, Caroline, who for thirty-nine years served as librarian for the Indiana Historical Society in Indianapolis.

The political mastermind behind measures to purify the state's ballot and one of the state's most respected historians was born on 12 April 1855 in Lawrenceburg, Indiana, the third of five children (four others had died in childhood) raised by Jacob and Harriet Louisa (Tate) Dunn. Dunn's father, Jacob Piatt Dunn, Sr., was the son of Isaac Dunn, one of the first settlers in the Whitewater valley. A judge, bank president, businessman, and postmaster in Lawrenceburg, Isaac Dunn often, after traveling to New Orleans on business matters, returned home on foot. Jacob Piatt Dunn, Sr., a cattle trader for a time up and down the Ohio River and a lifelong Democrat, was one of many who traveled to California in 1849 seeking his fortune in the goldfields. On 16 May 1849 Dunn and thirteen other men started on an eventual five-month-long trip West via ox team. "They met with great difficulties, suffering and destitution," John H. B. Nowland said of the party in a sketch of Dunn for an 1876 publication on prominent Indianapolis citizens. Dunn returned to Lawrenceburg in the spring of 1854, moving his family to a farm on the Ohio River. In the summer of 1861 he moved his family north to Indianapolis, where he opened a slaughterhouse and pork-packing business in partnership with James McTaggert. In the fall of 1864 he sold his interest in the pork firm and went into real estate work, a profession he followed until his death on 21 November 1890.[2]

A pious man, Dunn, Sr., upon his death, was lauded by the Meridian Street Methodist Episcopal Church of Indianapolis, where he had long been a member. "Brother Dunn was in every relation of life a character to be imitated and admired," read a memorial tribute adopted by the church. "His religious convictions being the result of candid thought and based upon a rational and intelligent faith, his religious life was symmetrical in all its parts."[3] The onetime prospector, who retained investments in some Colorado silver mines, made it a point to instill the same high degree of religious faith in his children, especially when it came to such matters as the morality of alcohol. On 2 April 1872 seventeen-year-old Jacob Piatt Dunn, Jr., and his siblings signed an agreement among themselves to abstain from drinking

Indianapolis in 1862, Washington Street looking east

or using "as a beverage any intoxicating liquors either distilled or fermented and for the faithful maintenance of this obligation relying for aid on Divine Providence we pledge to each other our word and honor."[4]

After attending private schools for several years, Dunn entered the public schools in Indianapolis in 1867. Four years later he was sent by his parents for further education to Earlham College in Richmond, Indiana, where he graduated in 1874 with a bachelor's degree in science. Life at the small Quaker institution of higher learning was filled with the same moral fervor the young man had experienced in the Dunn household in Indianapolis. Reminiscing about his days at Earlham during a meeting of the Society of Indiana Pioneers, Dunn noted that during his time there the college refused to allow any musical instruments on campus. "In three years I heard but one song in a religious service," he recalled. One Sunday during the church service a young

EARLHAM COLLEGE, RICHMOND,IND.

Earlham College, Richmond, Indiana, founded by the Religious Society of Friends (Quakers) in 1847

woman sang one verse of "Rock of Ages" all by herself. "It caused more discussion than any other event while I was there."[5]

His religious upbringing left its mark on Dunn. "There is nothing that affects a human life so much as a fervent, deep-seated belief, whether it concern religion or politics, or anything else," he said.[6] Dunn's religious upbringing fits a pattern shared by many Progressive Era men and women. In his study of one hundred of the first generation of American Progressives born between 1854 and 1874, Robert Morse Crunden found that they "absorbed the severe, Protestant moral values of their parents," but instead of entering the ministry, these educated men and women turned to new professions like academia, journalism, law, politics, and social work. "In each of these careers," Crunden noted, "they could become preachers urging moral reform on institutions as well as individuals."[7]

Dunn's moral fervor was tempered with a ready wit and evenhanded disposition. Russel Seeds, who worked with

Earlham College

Earlham College's class of 1874. Seated left to right: Jacob Piatt Dunn, Jr., Ruth Hinshaw, William F. Clawson, Esther A. White, and James B. Unthank. Standing left to right: William W. Jones, John R. White, Oliver H. Bogue, Edwin Horney, and Albert H. Votaw

Dunn on the *Indianapolis Sentinel* newspaper, called his fellow journalist the "most companionable man I ever knew." That opinion was shared by Laura Smith, an apprentice on the *Sentinel* staff who later worked for the *Indianapolis Star*. Along with his willingness to offer advice to a novice in the journalism profession, Smith was struck with Dunn's "quaint, quizzical humor" and "equitable temperament." She described him as "serene and deliberate amid verbal quarrels. I do not remember of ever seeing him lose his temper or break forth in anger no matter how hot the political dispute." Demarchus Brown, state librarian from 1906 to 1926, noted that although the two men did not always agree on every issue, he admired the manner in which Dunn was "always willing to discuss any question and the broad-minded attitude he took."[8]

Dunn did find time for more secular matters while at Earlham, becoming a leading figure in the Ionian Society, the campus's all-male literary society. The aim of the Ionian Society, which had merged with another Earlham literary group, the Hesperian Junto, in 1857, was for "cultivating language and mingling conversational pleasantry with the sterner truths of Philosophy and Science, and for the extension of our information on all subjects calculated to improve the mind or ennoble human nature." Along with this higher purpose, the organization established an extensive library for its members' use.[9]

Along with providing Dunn with an outlet for his budding intellect, the Ionian Society, in his junior year, offered him the chance to exercise his talent for writing through its magazine, *The Earlhamite*. Founded in 1873, the monthly periodical, published in a magazine format, served as a combination student newspaper, alumni magazine, and literary journal. Contributors were students, staff, faculty, alumni, and others, including James Whitcomb Riley poems and Maurice Thompson stories. In its inaugural December 1873 issue, the publication noted that it would "be a regular messenger going out bearing tidings of the prosperity and vicissitudes of Earlham to its friends and supporters, and bringing all who have been associated here into communication with one another."[10]

The driving force behind the Earlham journal's founding was Edwin Horney of Cicero, Indiana, who served as the magazine's first editor. Writing about the origins of *The Earlhamite* to celebrate its twenty-first anniversary of publication, Dunn noted that Horney, a fellow Ionian Society member, conferred with him about his plans for starting the publication. "I remember that I wondered somewhat why he had consulted me, but I felt honored by the confidence," Dunn said. "Possibly that was why he did it, for he was a wise man, and in one way and another he had not only convinced all interested parties of the feasibility of the venture, but also won from them a hearty interest in it before he announced it publicly." At an 18 September 1873 Ionian Society meeting, members agreed to publish a monthly periodical and appointed a committee, on which Dunn served, to investigate the costs involved in such a venture.[11]

In Dunn's recollections about *The Earlhamite*'s early years, there exists some hints of a healthy competition between himself and Horney, a fellow upperclassman. As president of the Ionian Society in 1874, his senior year at Earlham, Dunn presided over a number of meetings where issues regarding the publication were discussed. "On some of this I disagreed with the editor-in-chief," Dunn said, "but he [Horney] always had strength enough with the society to carry his points, and deservedly so." Horney, who later worked as a school principal in California, earned Dunn's respect during their years together at Earlham. "He was a natural leader," Dunn observed of Horney, who died in 1877, "stern and courageous when necessary, gentle and kindhearted when it would serve as well, honest thoroughly, a good debater, and as logical as the laws of nature."

Dunn must already have earned some recognition for his writing talent at Earlham, as the magazine's literary editor, James B. Unthank, asked the young man from Indianapolis to join his staff. Dunn declined the offer because "the enterprise was new, every one was enthusiastic, and I knew that there would be 'copy' to throw at the birds." Although Dunn also carried a heavy class schedule, he did inform Unthank that he could call on him for an article if he was in dire need of copy, an offer the literary editor took Dunn up on only once.[12]

Later, after Dunn had graduated and moved on to law school at the University of Michigan, he did furnish *The Earlhamite* with a number of articles. These early works in Dunn's bibliography reveal both his proficiency as a writer and his instinct for spirited debate on any issue. Issues of the magazine in 1875 and 1876 featured a lengthy travelogue contributed by Dunn on a trip he and a friend took to see Mammoth Cave in Kentucky, one of the largest known caverns in the world. In the piece he skillfully evoked the fear induced by a prank gone wrong when Dunn and other young men in the tour went on ahead of the rest of their party on the way out of the cave. Hoping to surprise the others, they extinguished the lamps used to light their way only to discover that they had forgotten to bring along any matches. "It was a novel sensation and one that I expect to remember," Dunn wrote. "One is overwhelmed by the awful silence and the sense of utter helplessness, for it would be impossible to escape unaided. I believe that if a stranger of ordinary nerve were lost in a cave for two hours, and in the dark, it would drive him mad." Luckily for Dunn and his companions, only a half hour passed before the rest of the party finally came into view.[13]

For the April 1881 issue of Earlham's magazine, Dunn, responding to a previous item by W. Wickerson on reforming rules for spelling, revealed his aptitude for slicing away at the heart of an opponent's argument, a skill he perfected as a staff member on numerous newspapers throughout his career. Dunn objected to Wickerson's listing of numerous professors and other learned men who supported spelling reform. The use of such great names was not, in Dunn's opinion, any argument in its favor for three reasons. First, he noted that men who are great in one line often saw all things "from their own stand-point, and think the whole world is bettered by what betters their department." Secondly, men who are great in one line frequently take sides on questions "in regard to which they are no better posted than ordinary mortals." Finally, Dunn pointed out that

Chestnut Street, Leadville, Colorado, July 1879

there "has never been any lunacy promulgated in the world which has not had some 'alleged' great men as supporters."[14]

Dunn was one of ten people in Earlham's graduating class of 1874. While the rest of the graduates indicated that they were to pursue careers in teaching or medicine, Dunn was the only one to choose the field of law, journeying to Ann Arbor to study at the University of Michigan. After receiving his law degree from the university in 1876, Dunn returned to Indianapolis and continued his studies with the prestigious local firm of McDonald & Butler. The young lawyer made a good impression on one of the firm's partners, John M. Butler. In an 11 March 1879 letter of introduction to former Civil War general and *Ben-Hur* author Lew Wallace, Butler described Dunn as a trustworthy man, a good lawyer, and a person possessing an understanding of business—"a gentleman in every sense of the word."[15] The rigors of law, however, were no match for the lure of the untamed West. In 1879 Dunn and his brothers left the Hoosier State for Colorado to look after their father's silver mine investments and to try their luck at prospecting. Just a year earlier there had been a rush to Leadville, Colorado, with the discovery of large quantities of the precious metal. "There are a great many strangers here, 'tender-feet' like myself," Dunn wrote

Harrison Avenue, Leadville, Colorado, 1879

a friend back in Indianapolis from Silver Cliff, Colorado, "who have come to seek their fortune. If half of us find it, we will carry off the State bodily."[16]

He discovered, however, that the life of a prospector in Colorado's mountains was hard and expensive. Just obtaining supplies proved to be a major undertaking. As one history of Colorado noted, profiteering in the area "seemed the rule, not the exception." Hay, for example, sold for two hundred dollars a ton during the winter season, foodstuffs cost four times more than in Denver, and Leadville shopkeepers could expect to make a fifteen hundred dollar profit on a single barrel of whiskey. Fortunes were also made in the hills of Colorado. Between 1879 and 1889, approximately eighty-two million dollars worth of silver was extracted and shipped from the Leadville area.[17]

The junior Dunn failed to strike it rich, but he did mine a collection of humorous stories about his adventures. On one prospecting trip into the mountains Dunn had camped near a stream and had gone to sleep only to awake at 10 P.M. that night nearly frozen. "Moved up nearer fire. Woke up 11 P.M., fire out; frozen to death; ditto at 12, 1, 2, 2:30, 3, 3:30, 4, 4:30, 5." In the morning he found that his burro had wandered from camp, and he spent a considerable time navigating the mountain's treacherous slopes to track it down. "The man who wrote 'Not for gold nor precious stones would I sell my mountain home,'" Dunn said, "was either a greenbacker or some other idiot who had never seen a mountain. I shall not go out of my way to climb mountains any more. If one approaches me I will defend myself, but I seek no trouble with them."[18]

Dunn also had some trouble getting accustomed to the differences between the West and his Indiana home. For example, there was not an inch of ground in Colorado that did not slope in some direction. "An old-timer told me that he went down into the plains for a couple of weeks last summer, and while there had to wear a stilt on one foot and sleep on a house-roof," Dunn said. Bothersome too were the strange animals he observed—white quails with pink eyes, blackbirds with white eyes, fish equipped with scales that cannot be removed, and tiny (compared to those in the East and Midwest) squirrels. "I saw a bumble-bee last week, and he looked so old-fashioned and natural that I wanted to shake hands with him," Dunn remarked in a 4 July 1879 newspaper article for the *Indianapolis Saturday Herald*. He also had trouble with a gang of mountain rats that devoured his provisions and the lining of his hat and were just about to eat the hobnails from his boots when he picked up his revolver and fired. Unfortunately, the rats escaped without injury; the same could not be said of Dunn's spirit lamp. After the incident the young prospector resolved to put away his handgun as it weighed too much to carry comfortably on the trail. He did, however, dream of a day when he could lure a mountain rat "down into some *mesa* where there is nothing in range but prairie dogs and cactuses, and then—ha! ha! revenge! I will shoot him with a club."[19]

These various troubles failed to diminish Dunn's rapture with his new surroundings. The thin air in Colorado's high elevations seemed to be affecting his mind, making him almost giddy. Dunn particularly remembered one occasion when he was climbing along the side of a mountain with a pickax slung over his shoulder and happened to spy three deer. He goes on to report:

> They saw me at the same time and started to run around me. I, with a "zeal but not according to knowledge," started to head them off. After I had run for about a mile it occurred to me that they were out of sight. In my excitement I had forgotten to watch them. I do not think they run any harder than I did, but there seems to be an element of speed about a deer that I do not possess. I carry a stout rope with me now, and when I see a deer, I tie myself to the nearest tree.[20]

He never did strike it rich through prospecting, but Dunn discovered something far more important, trades that sustained him for the rest of his life: journalism and history.[21] While in Colorado Dunn loved to hear tales from old-time prospectors, whom he called "glorious liars." These men often would "collar the unsuspecting 'tenderfoot' and stuff him till his mind is in the condition of a Thanksgiving turkey, and he goes off to retail their statements and get a reputation for their utter unreliability," Dunn noted.[22] It was also while in Colorado that the Hoosier native became fascinated with Native American lore and history. Inspired in part by the appearance in 1881 of Helen Hunt Jackson's *A Century of Dishonor*, an indictment of whites for their unjust treatment of Native Americans, he began to collect information on the clashes between white and Indian cultures, which motivated him to write what became the book *Massacres of the Mountains: A History of the Indian Wars of the Far West, 1815–1875.*

Along with starting him on the path to his career as a historian, his time in Colorado also gave Dunn a chance to exercise what a fellow Indiana historian, James A. Woodburn, described as "a versatile mind and a facile pen" through his work on a number of newspapers in the state.[23] Dunn contributed articles to the *Denver Tribune-Republican*, *Leadville Chronicle*, *Maysville Democrat*, and *Rocky Mountain News*. While covering city government for the *Denver Tribune-Republican*, Dunn came face-to-face with a problem he would make his life's work to solve—political corruption.

According to Dunn's account, on the Denver city council there were eight members who essentially ran the community. "Anybody who wanted anything from the city had to buy those eight members," he recalled. In one instance involving the C. B. & O. Railroad, which was attempting to build a line into the city, an ordinance the railroad wanted passed surprisingly faced opposition from all but one of the "Big Eight" council members. Running across the railroad's attorney, Dunn reported the following conversation:

> "Your ordinance seems to have hard sledding."
> "Yes," he responded grimly.
> "I understand there hasn't been a square divvy," I suggested.
> He smiled sweetly and turned away. At the next Council meeting the ordinance passed without opposition, and the story was in everybody's possession. The spokesman of the "Big Eight" had been approached and after negotiation had agreed to get the ordinance through for $5,000. The money had been paid to him, and he had

Denver, Colorado, circa 1880s

coolly appropriated all of it. The railroad company could not complain that its bribery had not been carried out as agreed. All it could do was to buy the other seven members independently.[24]

During Dunn's early days in the field, history was, as Richard Hofstadter noted, "the prerogative either of leisure-class gentlemen of commanding means or of a few hardy spirits . . . who had the energy for other enterprises as well as history."[25] In pursuing a dual interest in history and journalism, Dunn followed a path first blazed in the Hoosier State by the "Father of Indiana History," John B. Dillon, who wrote the respected *History of Indiana* (1843), worked as editor of the *Logansport Canal Telegraph*, and served as state librarian.[26] It was a trail also followed by Dunn's contemporaries, George S. Cottman, founder of the *Indiana Magazine of History* and author of frequent historical articles for Indianapolis newspapers; Claude G. Bowers, Indianapolis journalist, orator, and diplomat; and Albert J. Beveridge, Republican United States senator. Nationally, Dunn's role as an amateur historian involved in politics paralleled, but failed to match, the careers of men such as Theodore Roosevelt and Woodrow Wilson.[27]

Dunn returned to Indianapolis in 1884, wiser in the ways of politics and faced with the problem of making a living. Although he resumed the practice of law, he found time to visit the Indiana State Library and its collection of government documents in order to obtain the necessary material to complete his *Massacres of the Mountains* book, which was published in 1886 by Harper & Brothers of New York. "He was among the first historians of this subject," noted one scholar of Dunn's life, "to base his narrative on government documents, which he used extensively."[28] Dunn also drew upon the friendships he had made while in Colorado, exchanging a number of letters with witnesses to the events he described in the book. For his efforts, the young historian received 10 percent of the retail price of the book ($3.75) for every copy sold.[29]

In *Massacres of the Mountains*, Dunn attempted to, as he put it, "search out the true causes, the actual occurrences, and the exact results of the leading Indian troubles of modern years, leaving the credit or the blame to fall to whatever individual or whatever policy it may belong." Although he claimed to have "no theory to support" with his work, Dunn, showing the reforming instincts he honed in later life, argued against the government's policy of concentrating Indians on reservations, claiming there was not "a single instance of benefit resulting from an enforced removal—not one in which the fair presumption is not that the Indians would have done as well or better in their native homes."[30]

The young historian called for a policy of kindness and fairness toward the Indian, tempering justice with both religion and education. In arguing against the forced removal policy, however, Dunn patronizingly claimed that the worst result from such a policy was its hindrance to civilizing Native Americans. "If the Indian is to be civilized," he said, "he must first be brought into a complacent state of mind." For Dunn, it was absurd to begin the work of civilizing the Indian population by an act of harshness, i.e., the forced removal from native lands, that would be "felt longer and more keenly than anything else imaginable."[31]

The book received excellent reviews from newspapers around the country. Readers, advised the *Denver Tribune-Republican,* a newspaper for which Dunn worked for nearly a year, should disregard the book's rather misleading title, which suggested a sensational account involving bloody battles. "It is nothing of the kind," the newspaper said. "It is a historical work of great value, written in excellent style, and of a high literary tone." A reviewer from the *New York Examiner* said that if a copy of Dunn's book could be placed in the hands of every member of Congress, and if they could be made to read the work, "we should have more intelligent legislation on the Indian question, and no more Indian wars." The *Boston Globe* echoed other reviewers when it commended the Hoosier author for acting as a "faithful historian," letting the facts speak for themselves and relating them to the reader as an impartial observer. Closer to home, the *Indianapolis News* marveled at Dunn's "exhaustive" research and noted that the writer was not afraid "to hit where he thinks it deserved, and an occasional touch of sarcasm adds an agreeable spice," a spice Dunn used often in his subsequent writings.[32]

Massacres of the Mountains also received a positively glowing recommendation from another amateur historian, Theodore Roosevelt. A few years after Dunn's book had appeared, Roosevelt wrote Dunn that in conducting some studies he had occasion to reread *Massacres of the Mountains.* "I have been struck," said the future president, "with its absolute fairness and incisive truthfulness that I can not forebear writing to express my appreciation." Roosevelt went on to opine that Dunn's work would serve "as one of our standards."[33]

The two amateur historians later suffered a falling out of sorts over one of Indiana's notable figures, George Rogers Clark. In writing his book *The Winning of the West,* Roosevelt had criticized what he called the "small western historians" who damaged Clark's reputation by calling him the "Hannibal of the West" and the "Washington of the

Theodore Roosevelt

West" in their writings. Dunn pointed out, however, that the "small western historian" who had given Clark the title "Hannibal of the West" was, in fact, John Randolph of Virginia. The Hoosier historian went on to lament that Roosevelt was "not sufficiently acquainted with ancient history to know that the title was peculiarly apt." Like Hannibal, who crossed the Alps in the dead of winter and struck Rome by surprise, Dunn noted that Clark had maneuvered through the flooded fields of Illinois and Indiana in the dead of winter to strike the British unexpectedly at Vincennes. "It is the element of the surprising and unexpected that is associated with the name of Hannibal by classical writers and speakers. If John Randolph were alive today," he continued, "he might possibly refer to Mr. Roosevelt as The Hannibal of Oyster Bay."[34]

His work on the western clashes between Native Americans and settlers helped Dunn obtain an advanced degree. In November 1885 the Earlham College board of trustees accepted a thesis from Dunn, which became his book *Massacres of the Mountains*, and awarded him a master of science degree. At that time, at Earlham and at many American universities in the Midwest, the "line between the Master's degree based on a planned program and the honorary degree was ill defined."[35] An Earlham graduate who had been out of school for three years could receive a master's degree by either passing an examination upon a subject sanctioned by the faculty or by presenting a satisfactory thesis.

Dunn's success with *Massacres of the Mountains* caught the attention of the publishing firm Houghton Mifflin, which asked him to write the Indiana volume for its *American Commonwealths* series. In researching his book Dunn turned to such sources as the Library of Congress, the Bureau of American Ethnology, the Canadian archives, the Indiana State Library, and the Indianapolis Public Library. As far as Indiana sources were concerned, Dunn complained that in the existing written history of Indiana at that time there had been "so little citation of authorities that it has become almost impossible to distinguish those statements which are founded on authority from those whose basis is mere conjecture."[36]

The result of Dunn's research, *Indiana: A Redemption from Slavery*, published in 1888, saw the author concentrate his efforts on exploring the question of slavery in the Indiana Territory, which, according to Dunn, was the key issue in the area up to the time of statehood in 1816. "It [slavery] was the tap-root of our political growth,—the great central matter of controversy to which all other questions were subordinate," he said. "In short, it made a quarter of a century of our political history, and, at the end of that time, left the people of Indiana more strongly opposed to the institution of slavery than they ever could have been without it."[37]

By focusing so completely on the slavery question, Dunn managed to bring his 450-page history of the state only up to

1816, leaving seventy-two years of Hoosier heritage unwritten (a lapse he later rectified in a 1905 revision). His single-minded devotion to detailing the issue of slavery in Indiana troubled many reviewers. According to the *New York Times*, readers of Dunn's book would be disappointed. "The work is not what it seems to be, it is not what other volumes in the same series have been, nor is it what it ought itself to have been," the *Times* said. Although Dunn failed in some areas, for example, offering a complete outline of the state's political history, a reviewer for *The Nation* said the author succeeded in skillfully exploring the slavery question with painstaking detail and noted that Dunn described the lives of the French pioneers in the territory with "rare grace."[38]

In its review of *Indiana: A Redemption from Slavery*, the *New York Times* had also denigrated Dunn's writing style as "severely plain and colorless," adding that the author's over-reliance on facts made the book "rather hard reading" for the general public. Although the work does lack the liveliness of his later publications, here and there Dunn's passion for history shines through. Seemingly obscure details delighted the historian. In one example he noted that when British commander Henry Hamilton captured Vincennes he seized all the liquor and announced to the community his intention to destroy all billiard tables in the town. "Think of it!" Dunn exclaimed. "Billiard tables on the Wabash in 1778! What a time they must have had . . . on those vast expanses of green cloth, with dead cushions, uneven balls, and crooked cues!"[39]

Through the years other historical publications flowed from Dunn's pen, including *Documents Relating to the French Settlements on the Wabash* (1894), *Men of Progress* (1899), *True Indian Stories* (1909), the two-volume *Greater Indianapolis* (1910), *Memorial and Genealogical Record of Representative Citizens of Indiana* (1912), and the five-volume state history *Indiana and Indianans* (1919). Some of these works were produced by Dunn more as a means of making a living than as serious historical research. For the biographical publication *Memorial and Genealogical Record,* for example, B. F. Bowen & Company of Indianapo-

Indiana authors playing card depicting Dunn as author of *Indiana: A Redemption from Slavery* and *Massacres of the Mountains*

lis required in its contract with Dunn permission to use the historian's name on a printed prospectus and on order blanks describing the book as an incitement to potential buyers. Also, the historian was to sign letters "introducing representatives of the Company to different individuals throughout the State, and assist in giving references and such information as may be of use to the proposed work from time to time." Apparently Dunn's name on a work translated into sales for a publisher.[40]

The local and state histories produced by Dunn, *Greater Indianapolis* and *Indiana and Indianans*, are both marked by a refreshing lack of boosterism on the writer's part and a dedicated effort to document his sources through footnotes. He presents the history of the state and city he loved warts and all. In relating the city's creation, Dunn offers a less than reverential anecdote involving Stephen Ludlow, one of the commissioners charged by the state legislature with finding suitable land for a new state capital. Returning to his home in Lawrenceburg, Ludlow bragged to William Tate, a young mechanic from Boston, about how the site selected was "as level as a barn floor." When Tate asked Ludlow what the community would then do for drainage, the commissioner, briefly nonplussed, finally responded: "Well, I'll be d----d. Nobody but a Yankee would ever have thought of that."[41]

And notwithstanding his often, at best, patronizing attitude toward African Americans, Dunn, in *Greater Indianapolis*, gives an objective overview involving a 4 July 1845 incident where a black man was beaten to death by a white mob under circumstances, he noted, "that would have disgraced any rowdy settlement in the country."[42] Also, as someone who participated in a number of Indianapolis's and Indiana's leading political battles, Dunn was in a unique position to offer an insider's view of history, which makes for entertaining and informative reading. Both of these works still stand today, as Lana Ruegamer notes, as "indispensable sources for workers in Indiana history."[43]

In conducting his research for these works, Dunn was always meticulous, adopting a hands-on approach. Karl Detzer, who grew up in Fort Wayne, Indiana, during the turn of the century, knew the historian as a friend of his mother. Detzer remembered Dunn as a "gentle, hulking, pipe-smoking, seemingly very old man . . . who strained tremendously interesting conversation through a mustache of heroic proportions." The two often explored northeast Indiana for artifacts, and through Dunn, Detzer learned that history did not merely consist of facts printed in books, but instead consisted of "a swamp where your feet sank into deep Indiana muck; or a sandbar across a creek; or a trail winding through willow thickets to what looked like an ordinary low hump of earth; or a faint, narrow path zigzagging up to a high point where . . . you saw down below, not just the prosperous new red barns with their Mail Pouch Tobacco signs, but the glorious past that helped erect them."[44]

Also noting Dunn's thoroughness when it came to research was his daughter, Caroline. To her, her father seemed to be "forever rushing around trying to see some old Indianapolis person before he died in order to get his recollections of early days."[45] Dunn's great "intellectual curiosity," said his daughter, marked him for life as a person who is "always reaching for a dictionary or encyclopedia, trying to identify a new flower . . . or running down some historical item!" Calling Dunn a "delightful father," Caroline also remembered that he often took his daughters and other children in the neighborhood with him for walks in the country, where he indulged in his hobby of mushroom collecting, always returning home with a couple of sacks full of the fungi. For his extensive studies on the language of the Miami Indians, Caroline noted, her father made a number of trips to Oklahoma to talk to members of the tribe and also consulted with Miami interpreters still in Indiana. "Meanings and derivations, grammar and changes in word forms, had for

IHS, C6577

(Left to right) Eleanor and Caroline Dunn as children

him the fascination of a puzzle or problem to be worked out,"
she observed. Her father also was "keenly aware of the need
of preserving a record of the Indian languages before they
should be lost through disuse." [46]

Dunn preserved a bit of the Miami language by anoint-
ing each of his daughters with Miami names. Caroline recalled that her younger sister Eleanor's Miami name was
Pa-pin-djin-wa, which meant "always falling down."[47]
Dunn often displayed his well-known wit with his children, especially when they were away from home, vacationing in Leland, Michigan. For years Caroline carefully
saved the color postcards sent to her in Leland by her father. These postcards often featured color cartoons of two
small girls involved in a variety of situations upon which
Dunn commented. In one featuring children preparing for
church, Dunn wrote: "When Caroline goes to Sunday
School she carries pennies for the little heathen in her
pocket book. The heathen can use the pennies in buying

IHS, C6576

The Dunn home at 915 North Pennsylvania Street in Indianapolis

chewing gum and peanuts, and paying their tariff taxes. If they did not get the pennies they would have to eat missionaries."[48]

Dunn's interest in history, he acknowledged, had been held through the years "chiefly by the detective problems it presents—the puzzles, great and small, that confront the historical student on all sides." If he were to teach a class in historical research he would instruct his students to follow the maxim set by Monsieur Lecog, a detective in a French mystery series: "In any mysterious case, suspect what seems probable; examine carefully what seems improbable, or even impossible." Dunn went on to counsel his would-be students that if there is "a single fact, of which you are absolutely certain, which is inconsistent with your theory, there must be something wrong with the theory." The one, constant factor in human history, no matter what nationality or time period, according to Dunn, was human nature. He went on to say:

IHS, KC7260

The Indiana Historical Society presented these candleholders and clock to Dunn and his wife Charlotte as a wedding present

The things that are subject to change are manners, customs,
knowledge, beliefs, moral standards, and the like. Hence, be cautious about applying the standards of today to other ages. Put
yourself as nearly as possible in the place of the characters you are
studying, and estimate probabilities from their point of view.[49]

His relentless quest to seek out knowledge and impart it
to others could be more than a little exasperating to Dunn's
colleagues. David Laurance Chambers, president of the Indianapolis publishing firm Bobbs-Merrill, and like Dunn a
member of the Indianapolis Literary Club, remembered one
occasion when the Hoosier historian thoroughly puzzled
famed novelist Henry James. According to Chambers, during a visit to Indianapolis James was the guest of honor at
a special luncheon at the University Club "where he
[James] was expected to do all the talking. But Jake Dunn
took over and Henry didn't have a chance. Jake expatiated
on his experiences while paying his way through college."
After the luncheon James turned to Chambers and asked:
"Who was the extraordinary fellah who had been a
waiter?"[50]

On occasion Dunn's passion for his research, and the
paths on which it could lead him, could even disturb his wife
of thirty-two years, Charlotte Elliott (Jones) Dunn. Married
on 23 November 1892, the couple lived for much of their
married life in a house at 915 North Pennsylvania Street
that had been built in 1868 by Charlotte's father, Aquilla
Jones, a part owner of the Indianapolis wholesale firm of
Jones, McKee & Company. The couple met when they both
had parts in an amateur theatrical being staged at the Indianapolis Propylaeum Club. Before her marriage to Dunn,
Charlotte Jones served as a secretary to May Wright Sewall
and helped the Indianapolis educator, suffragist, and club
woman with her work at the Classical School for Girls and
the development of the Propylaeum. Like her husband,
Charlotte played an active role in a number of Indianapolis
organizations, including the Fortnightly Literary Club, the
Portfolio Club, and the Society of Indiana Pioneers. In 1912
Gov. Thomas R. Marshall, who would work closely with Jacob Dunn on reforming the Indiana constitution, appointed

Charlotte a member of the Indiana Women's Prison board of trustees, a post she held until 1937. After Jacob Dunn's death in 1924, Charlotte became curator at the Propylaeum, home to the Indianapolis Woman's Club, where she worked until her retirement in July 1944.[51] By all accounts the Dunns had a happy marriage. Charlotte, nicknamed "Sharlie" by her husband, however, often worried when Dunn made trips away from the comforts of home. In a letter sent to her husband in Haiti, where he was exploring for manganese in 1922, Charlotte told him about a strange incident that had occurred while he was away. "The morning after Christmas . . . I was awakened with a start about six thirty and heard you call out just as plainly as if you were in your own room—'Oh, Sharlie,'" she wrote. "It made me quite uncomfortable for a time, and yet, when nothing happened, I put it out of my mind."[52]

These occasional long separations while Dunn pursued his historical inquiries never seemed to diminish Charlotte's affection for her husband. "It seems to me," she wrote Dunn in Haiti, "that you and your retinue, when you start out prospecting, must look not unlike Don Quixote and his Sancho Panza! Your dun-colored steed and your long, thin legs! But I hope you may have all the good luck you desire, as well as the adventure."[53]

Dunn himself could become exasperated at being the only male in a household that included his wife, two daughters, his mother-in-law, and sister-in-law (a son born to the Dunns in 1894 drowned while the family was vacationing in Nantucket in 1902). Although an affectionate father, Dunn did sometimes wish for a little peace and quiet. On one occasion his vacationing daughters wrote informing him that they were thinking of coming home a week early. Dunn, who had just seen his wife off on a trip and was preparing for a quiet vacation at home alone, begged his daughters to "pity the sorrows of a poor old man" and continue their vacation. In a speech titled "A Modern Martyr," Dunn slyly referred to his situation when he asked his audience if they had known men who "while striving to do right, have fallen victims to the fury of scientific housecleaning, and who look

Eleanor (sitting on trunk) and Caroline Dunn near the railroad tracks while on vacation at Plum Lake, Wisconsin

fondly forward to an eternal home where books, papers and other possessions are never disturbed or lost."[54]

Finding documents and other materials on which to base his historical work proved to be an even tougher task for

Dunn than finding minerals in the Caribbean, especially when he attempted to gain access to archives in the East. Hearing about a large collection of documents relating to the Northwest Territory located in the State Department in Washington, D.C., Dunn, during Democratic president Grover Cleveland's first term in office, used his friendship with Indiana senator Joseph E. McDonald, in whose law firm he had worked and who knew Secretary of State Thomas Francis Bayard, to secure permission to examine the material. "Notwithstanding my formidable introduction, I came near having to fight for everything I got," said Dunn. It seems that the librarian assisting Dunn was a "scion of a notable New England family." The librarian insisted on watching the Hoosier historian "like a hawk; and the way he glared at me when, on being informed that they did not have something I wanted, I insisted in looking for myself—which I had discovered was the only way of making sure of anything at Washington—was literally and truly fierce."[55]

Dunn had almost as much difficulty pursuing his historical research when he returned to Indiana. Appalled by the difficulty in obtaining state records, and the lack of care accorded to those materials already in hand, Dunn joined with

Dunn relaxes with some female friends on an outing to Morgan County, Indiana, circa 1910

Indiana senator Joseph E. McDonald

two other men, William H. English, Democratic nominee for vice president in 1880, and Republican judge Daniel Wait Howe, both respected amateur historians in their own right, to revitalize a comatose private organization—the Indiana Historical Society, which had been in existence since 1830 but had held no meetings since 1879. In doing so, Dunn also played a major role in obtaining from the normally tight-fisted Indiana legislature increased funding for a small state agency, the Indiana State Library. The onetime prospector may have come up empty making his fortune in the West, but he had discovered in his hometown institutions that enriched his professional and private life for years to come.

2

Laboring for Indiana History

ON THE FOURTEENTH ANNIVERSARY OF INDIANA'S ENTRY INTO the Union as the nineteenth state, the evening of 11 December 1830, a "large and respectable meeting" was held at the Marion County Courthouse that included some of the most distinguished figures in the state's and Indianapolis's early history—prominent Indianapolis attorney Calvin Fletcher; Indiana Supreme Court judges Isaac Blackford and Jesse L. Holman; future Indiana governors David Wallace and James Whitcomb; Indiana state treasurer Samuel Merrill; and more than half of the members of the General Assembly. The group had come together to consider forming a historical society for the state of Indiana. Finding themselves in agreement on that intention, the group appointed a committee of seven gentlemen, which included Wallace, Blackford, Holman, and John H. Farnham, an attorney who played an important part in the Society's infancy, to draft a constitution for the new organization. After retiring from the assembly for only a few minutes, the committee came back with a draft of a constitution that was speedily adopted. Under the document, the objects of the new Historical Society of Indiana (later known as the Indiana Historical Society) were "the collection of all materials calculated to shed light on the natural, civil, and political history of Indiana, the promotion of useful knowledge, and the friendly and profitable intercourse of such citizens of the state as are disposed to promote the aforesaid objects."[1]

In spite of this auspicious beginning, the Society suffered severe growing pains in its early years. The institution, which had been chartered through an act of the General Assembly on 10 January 1831, received the biggest blow to its continued success when Farnham died in 1833 during an Indianapolis cholera epidemic. The Society's activities went through numerous fits and starts throughout the nineteenth century. "Its existence," noted one official, "has been very quiet—so quiet at times as to suggest death."[2] Inactive from 1835 to 1848, the Society held only a few meetings between 1848 and 1853 and endured a long period of doldrums from 1859 to 1873. Although the group revived for a bit in the late 1870s, it again went into hibernation as of 1879. Only through the efforts of Dunn and his fellow amateur historians did the Society again see the light of day.[3]

In 1886 Dunn was one of several Indianapolis gentlemen who had agreed to unite to form an association whose purpose would be to preserve Indiana historical materials, which were of vital need to historians such as Dunn,

IHS, C7159

Daniel Wait Howe

IHS, C7157

William H. English

William H. English, and Daniel Wait Howe. One of the men asked to join this new organization was Maj. Jonathan W. Gordon, an important Indianapolis lawyer made famous through his service as a defense attorney at treason trials held in the state during the Civil War. According to Dunn, it was Gordon, a Society member, who suggested that instead of organizing a new group, the old Indiana Historical Society should be reorganized. Dunn and the others were more than happy to oblige.[4]

At a special meeting held on the evening of 8 April 1886 in the Indiana State Library's rooms on the southeast corner of Tennessee and Market Streets, a group composed of Society members and the new blood successfully reorganized the Society. At that meeting Dunn was selected to be the group's recording secretary, a post he served in until his death; English was elected president; and Howe became third vice president. The 1886 organization, however, was quite a different one from the 1830 model. In its new incarnation the Society moved from an open membership to an elite institution, with members elected by secret ballot that required a three-fourths majority. This membership requirement, Lana Ruegamer notes in her history of the Society, imitated "other prestigious gentlemen's clubs in Indianapolis, like the Indianapolis Literary Club and the Contemporary Club."[5] Some of those who were able to survive this new standard and become Society members in the coming months included Hoosier author Maurice Thompson, Indiana University president David Starr Jordan, Franklin judge D. D. Banta, and former governor Albert G. Porter. To ensure that the Society's transformation would be complete, the "new" members approved a resolution at a special meeting held nine days after the Society had been revitalized that any of the old members who "fail to pay their dues for the current year within 30 days from this date be dropped from the rolls and be no longer members."[6] All of this worked to keep the institution's membership small. In fact, as of 1907 the Society had only eighty-nine members, a far cry from the approximately ten thousand-strong membership reported by the Society in 1996.

The newly revamped Society continued to be plagued by some of the same problems encountered by the old organization, especially when it came to finding suitable office space. "We have never been able to get a room where we could keep anything," Dunn reminisced at the first State Historical Conference in 1919. "We do not have the money to rent a room, and have never been able to keep a room in the State House or the [Marion County] Court House." Through his political connections, however, Dunn did obtain a small office, which was also used as a janitor's storeroom, for the Society in the Indianapolis City Hall. Since this area was kept unlocked for a number of years over the protests of Society officers, the group could not meet its original goal—preserving Indiana historical materials for use by researchers in years to come. Dunn had the solution. "The only way to save anything," he said, "is to put it into print as quickly as possible."[7]

As early as the original meeting when the Society was revitalized, Dunn had been pushing for the group to publish material on Indiana history. He introduced a resolution,

Indiana State Library

Jacob Piatt Dunn, Jr.

adopted by those assembled, authorizing the executive committee to contract on the Society's behalf "with any reliable
publishing firm for the publication of papers under the auspices of the Society; *provided,* that no cost or risk of publication shall fall on the Society."[8] Luckily for the Society, Indianapolis was the home of a very reputable publishing
house, the Bowen-Merrill Company (later Bobbs-Merrill),

publisher for such Hoosier literary giants as James Whitcomb Riley, the "Hoosier Poet," and Meredith Nicholson, author of the best-selling *The House of a Thousand Candles*. Under the arrangement between the Society and the publisher, Bowen-Merrill printed the Society's publications free of charge and supplied the organization with one hundred complimentary copies. Also, Bowen-Merrill paid the historical organization a 10 percent royalty if sales went above two hundred copies.[9]

The Society's publications program also benefited from having a person like Dunn on hand as a writer of articles and as a historical detective tracking down for publication Society minutes and papers read before the group during its first fifty-six years of existence. "At such a task of discovery and collection," said James A. Woodburn of Indiana University, who prepared a history of the Society's first one hundred years, "Dunn was an adept. He had a historical scent and could follow a trail to its source."[10] Dunn spent ten years in tracking down the necessary material, a "long and trying" search, he remembered. For example, a number of years passed before he could find any trace of a paper by John B. Dillon on the national decline of the Miami Indians. According to Dunn, tradition had it that the lecture had been printed in a Cincinnati newspaper. A search of the newspaper's files for the six months following the lecture's delivery failed to produce a copy. By chance English happened to come into possession of a fragment of the address, but it had no date or the name of the newspaper. Dunn discovered, however, that the type corresponded to that used by the *Cincinnati Gazette*. Upon further investigation, he found "on the back of the slip, where the columns slightly overlapped, the letters 't 28,' which were guessed to be the remnants of a date line, and could mean, of course, nothing but August 28. By this clue the article was easily found as printed some fifteen months after its delivery." Finally, in 1897, eleven years following the publication of Volume 2, featuring the new Society's early works, Volume 1 of the Society's *Publications* appeared, which included nearly all of its material from 1830 to 1886.[11]

Along with breathing new life into the Society, Dunn, with the aid of other Society members, also worked to improve another sadly neglected institution—the Indiana State Library. Created by the General Assembly in 1825, the state library, with the secretary of state also serving as state librarian, was at first for the exclusive use of the members of the legislature, secretaries and clerks of each house, officers of the different branches of the executive departments of the state government, judges of the federal district court, judges of the state supreme and circuit courts when in session in Indianapolis, and the United States district attorney. Books were allowed to be checked out for ten days, with fines levied at twenty-five cents for every day overdue. The legislature appropriated the sum of fifty dollars that first year both to purchase books and to bind pamphlets, after that the sum was reduced to thirty dollars a year.[12]

The secretary of state operated the library until 1841, when the legislature designated it as a separate agency and established the office of state librarian, a political office usually filled by the party that controlled the General Assembly. The political nature of the job caused considerable instability; from 1841 until the position was removed from the political process in 1897, twenty-one individuals held the state librarian post. Along with caring for the state's book collection, the state librarian also served as custodian of the statehouse and its grounds. When the legislature recessed, the state librarian had to dust and roll up the carpets in the rooms where the legislators had met and make sure that no livestock wandered onto the statehouse lawn. If, by any chance, the librarian loaned a book to a person not authorized to use the state library, he faced paying a fine anywhere from ten to one hundred dollars. All of these responsibilities fell upon a state employee paid the handsome annual sum of three hundred dollars.[13]

Although appropriations for binding and purchasing books never inched above four hundred dollars a year until the late 1880s, the state library proved to be, according to Dunn, "an influential factor in the intellectual life of the city." Works in the library were used by such luminaries as

Lew Wallace writing at his home in Crawfordsville, Indiana

onetime Indianapolis minister Henry Ward Beecher, who used the library's collections as an aid in editing the *Indiana Farmer and Gardener*, and Hoosier author Lew Wallace. As a young boy growing up in Indianapolis, Wallace often skipped the boredom of the schoolroom in order to sample the more exciting wares offered by the state library. "In the most impressionable period of my life," he writes in his autobiography, "I was introduced to Washington Irving and Fenimore Cooper, or more plainly, to their works; and I revelled in them, especially Cooper's, whose subjects were better adapted to my opening mind." For months and months after that discovery Wallace's "name figured on the receipt register of the library more frequently than any other."[14]

Over the years, however, the state library received less and less attention, as well as funding, from the General Assembly. With a reorganized and revitalized Society in the late 1880s, however, the library found a staunch ally. In 1887 a special Society committee that included as its mem-

bers English, Gen. John Coburn, superior court judge John
A. Holman, and United States district attorney Charles
Holstein presented to the legislature a request for space in
the new state capitol and funds to publish the executive
journal of the Indiana Territory. In addition, the committee
asked for increased appropriations on behalf of the state library, five thousand dollars the first year and two thousand dollars every year thereafter. Although the Society
did manage to win office space in the new capitol, its attempt to garner increased support for the state library
failed to make its way successfully through the legislative
process. The stage was set, however, for Dunn to work his
political magic on the library's behalf during the following
year.[15]

Along with the backing of the Society, which abandoned
its own wishes to wring fifteen hundred dollars a year from
the legislature, Dunn rounded up support for increased library funding (five thousand dollars for one year and two
thousand dollars per year thereafter for books and binding)
from other institutions. "Other state societies—the State
Board of Agriculture, Horticultural Society, Horse Breeders,
Sheep Breeders, Jersey Breeders, Short Horn Breeders,
Hog Breeders, Bee Keepers, etc., were glad to join in the
movement," said Dunn, "on condition that the literature of
their various lines be put in the library, and when the legislature met there was so strong an influence for the proposed
measure that it was readily adopted." Along with the increased funding for the library, the law established a purchasing board to oversee expenditures for the buying and
binding of books, increased the librarian's pay to fifteen
hundred dollars annually, provided one thousand dollars for
preparing a card catalog, and removed the requirement that
the librarian also serve as statehouse custodian. Democrats
in the legislature had another reason for supporting the
measure, as Dunn had agreed to take the position of librarian "and look after the interests of the Democratic party,
which I did for four years."[16]

During his two terms (April 1889 to April 1893) as state
librarian, Dunn set out to "put the library in presentable

condition and make reasonable additions to it."[17] Although untrained in library science, the amateur historian more than achieved his goal. In her history of the state library, Esther U. McNitt notes that Dunn's administration stands out for the way in which he was able to build up the collection "with standard and other valuable works along historical and other lines." Along with carefully selecting noteworthy books, pamphlets, and maps, Dunn also removed all duplicate volumes from the library's shelves and prepared a card catalog for use by library patrons. In fact, he did his job so well that the General Assembly, reasoning that enough had been accomplished, cut the library's annual appropriation from two thousand to one thousand dollars.[18] With the end of Dunn's second term as librarian, the legislature passed a new law placing the library's management under the State Board of Education, which acted as the State Library Board. Also, as of 1 April 1897 the power to select the state librarian was removed from the General Assembly and given to the Board of Education. By removing the library from politics, McNitt noted, the legislators hoped to prevent the frequent turnover of librarians, thus allowing the library to benefit by allowing it "to follow the same policy for a longer period."[19]

Before, during, and even after his terms as state librarian, Dunn played an important role in making free public libraries—institutions he considered "the most important educational agencies a commonwealth can have"—available to Hoosiers.[20] For years he had worked to revive the system of township libraries first established by the state as part of the school law of 1852. The law provided for a tax for two years of a quarter of a mill on the dollar, or twenty-five cents on one thousand dollars, and a poll tax of twenty-five cents, to be used to purchase books for township libraries. The tax for these institutions continued for another year under the revised school law of 1855. The tax raised $273,000 for the purchase of books for the township libraries, which amounted to approximately $290 to each township. By 1856 Caleb Mills, Indiana superintendent of public instruction and the state's leading advocate for common school education, declared that examining the circulation reports from these township libraries would convince even "the most skeptical that a one-quarter of a mill property and a twenty-five cents poll tax never accomplished so much for education in any other way."[21]

Unfortunately, an event occurred that, to Dunn's mind, almost turned people's attention away for good from the township libraries—the Civil War. "There was little thought of the future," he said of this period, "and less of the past. Everything was absorbed in the present." This state of affairs, he went on to say, was not consistent with "research and reflection," and the township libraries foundered. An attempt was made to bolster the libraries in 1865 with the General Assembly approving a tax of one-tenth of a mill on the dollar, or one cent on one hundred dollars, for their support. Funds meant for the township libraries, however, were used instead for the creation of a normal school at Terre Haute (now Indiana State University). "Left thus without any support," Dunn noted, "the libraries were of necessity doomed to continual deterioration." No books could be added, none replaced if worn out, nor could a book be rebound when needed, he added.[22]

Such a situation was anathema to Dunn. Along with his disgust over the waste of those books purchased through the original law, the historian, as he would with cleansing the ballot box, saw a moral responsibility in providing free public libraries to the people of Indiana, especially for Hoosier children. In talks before teachers, writers, and other groups, Dunn asked his audience to stop at any book stand in the state and examine the literature available to boys and girls. "It is simply astonishing how much evil can be purchased for five cents—enough to poison a mind—enough to ruin a life," he said. "Are the religious and moral elements of Indiana doing their duty so long as the State does not offer to the children in every neighborhood good reading matter without money and without price?"[23]

Dunn's agitation on the need for free public libraries finally paid off in 1899 with the creation by the General Assembly of the Indiana Public Library Commission. Dunn's voice on the issue had been joined by a chorus from a confederation of women's literary clubs. At its June 1897 meeting, the Indiana Union of Literary Clubs (IULC), which advocated the need for public libraries in its work, passed a resolution authorizing its president to appoint a committee to work with the Indiana Library Association (ILA) in writing for the creation of a State Library Commission (one of the members of that committee just happened to be Charlotte Dunn, Jacob Piatt Dunn's wife). Along with cooperation from the ILA, the IULC received help from the Indianapolis Commercial Club, the forerunner of the Indianapolis Chamber of Commerce. "I united with them," Dunn said of these efforts, "on condition that a provision for township libraries be included in the law."[24] The reformer got what he wanted.

During the 1899 legislative session, two bills were submitted to create an Indiana Public Library Commission, one from the ILA and one from the IULC. The main difference between the two bills was that the library association wanted to place the library commission under the control of the State Library Board, while the literary union sought an independent commission. A compromise was reached by having the IULC bill amended to allow the state librarian to be an ex officio secretary to the commission. Along with creating an Indiana Public Library Commission with three members appointed by the governor, the library bill appropriated three thousand dollars to inaugurate a system of traveling libraries and allowed any township, by vote, to initiate a tax of two cents on each one hundred dollars of property for maintaining a free public library. Dunn's dream had at last come true.[25]

Dunn was one of three people appointed to serve as members of the commission by Republican governor James A. Mount, along with Elizabeth C. Earl of Connersville and Joseph R. Voris of Bedford. At the group's first meeting on 11 April 1899 the commission members, who served without pay, elected Dunn as their president, a post he held until 1915. Almost immediately the commission started buying books to equip two types of traveling libraries: miscellaneous collections consisting of forty volumes each, which were similar in scope, and study libraries containing ten to fifteen books each on a specific subject. From having no traveling libraries in 1899, Indiana went in 1911 to having ten thousand volumes with an annual circulation throughout the state of twenty-three thousand. Also, the number of public libraries in the nineteenth state grew from a total of 57 in 1899, with only one librarian having library school training, to 197 public libraries, 163 special libraries, and 190 librarians with some library school training by 1916. So pleased was the legislature with the commission's work that it increased the appropriation for the organization's clerical expenses from five hundred dollars to one thousand dollars, as well as adding two thousand dollars for books and equipment.

Of course, as even Dunn himself admitted, the astonishing growth of libraries in the Hoosier State was not all due to the work of the commission. The development of libraries "would have been impossible," he said, but for the timely generosity of industrialist Andrew Carnegie, whose total gifts for establishing public libraries in Indiana amounted to more than two and a half million dollars. Still, the commission served a vital role in offering advice to communities on how to plan and organize library facilities. Also, the commission responded to the increased need for trained librarians for these new institutions. "The management of a library is a profession," noted William E. Henry, who as state librarian from 1897 to 1906 served on the commission, "and yet a little instruction . . . would enable a reasonably intelligent person, with the aid of the published text-books that are accessible, to manage a small library very satisfactorily." To meet this need the commission instituted library classes at its offices from 31 October to 7 November 1901 attended by thirteen persons. A library school, under the direction of Harriet L. Eaton, a graduate of the Pratt Library School, instructed twenty-eight Hoosiers connected with library work in the state the next year. For those not directly involved in library work, institutes were held at Indianapolis, New Albany, Peru, and

South Bend to discuss library topics and local library conditions. Henry noted that in each case the institute gave "a stimulus to interest in libraries."[26] In 1925 the commission and state library were merged and placed under the governance of the Indiana Library and Historical Board, appointed by the governor, which today continues to monitor the state library's operations.

Dunn's efforts to reinvigorate the Society, the Indiana State Library, and township libraries bore dividends that are still paying off for Hoosier citizens. And although he received little or no monetary compensation for this work, Dunn did learn some valuable lessons that he used in other reform efforts. As he pointed out during his battle to resurrect the township libraries, in America if "the people want anything, and say so, they get it." To reach that point, however, those interested in accomplishing change must overcome the public's lack of information and apathy on specific issues. "There must be talking done, and not a little of it," Dunn said. He would do a lot of talking in the years to come on a number of issues vital to Indiana.[27]

3

The Presidential Election of 1888 and the Australian Ballot Issue in Indiana

IN 1888 THE DEMOCRATIC STATE CENTRAL COMMITTEE'S LITER-ary bureau came under the control of a man who would use his considerable writing skills to promote the party's interests for years to come, Jacob Piatt Dunn, Jr. His efforts in that year's election caught the eye of the *New York Times*, which called Dunn "one of the leading young Democrats of the State, and but for the quiet tastes which lead him into literary work he might aspire to higher honors."[1] This marked the beginning of Dunn's long career as a "political man of letters," who earned much of his living as "a professional Democrat."[2] Along with his position as state librarian, other political jobs he held throughout his career included two terms (1904–6, 1914–16) as Indianapolis city controller and serving as chief deputy to Marion County treasurer Frank P. Fishback from 1910 to 1912. In 1902 Dunn made his only attempt at a major elective office when he ran as the Democratic nominee against Republican incumbent Jesse Overstreet for Indiana's Seventh Congressional District.

Although Dunn failed to unseat his GOP opponent—the Democrat tallied 20,933 votes as compared with Overstreet's total of 25,191—his campaign hit on a theme the historian used again and again in his battles for reform. Speaking before workers at John Rauch's Indianapolis cigar factory, Dunn argued that popular government was hopeless unless citizens acted to right injustices. "There is no wrong—no evil—that may not be remedied under our present form of government," he said, "if the people will but undertake it

Indiana State Library

Claude G. Bowers

Indiana State Library

Louis Ludlow

seriously." The best hope for any kind of representative form of government "lies in the determination of the people to act for their own best interests." If citizens neglected their duties, their government, no matter what form it might have, would be a failure, Dunn added.[3]

The partisan reformer's greatest opportunity to share his vision with Hoosiers came not as a Democratic candidate running for political office, but as a writer on the party's behalf. The bulk of Dunn's journalistic career in Indianapolis was spent writing for "party organs"—newspapers aligned with a particular political organization (in his case, the Democratic *Indianapolis Sentinel*, for which Dunn served as editor for a time). Newspapers during this period were often the public's only source for information about politics. Also, newspapers were allied more closely to political parties than they are today. "Roughly two-thirds . . . claimed connection with one of the two parties," according to Philip R. Vander-Meer, "an affiliation which not only determined their editorial policies but also shaped their reporting of events."[4] Indiana newspaper veteran and future Washington correspondent and congressman Louis Ludlow recalled that at the *Sentinel* office there existed one overriding dictate for guiding the staff: "Never err against the Democratic Party." Conversely, he continued, it was a matter of course that if "there was any erring to be done it should be done against the Republican Party."[5] Claude G. Bowers, a Democrat and self-trained Hoosier historian in his own right, also worked for the *Sentinel* for a time. Bowers maintained that the news stories contained in the partisan press, "while colored, deceived no one. With papers representing both parties, the public had the advantage of a debate, so important in a democracy." Bowers was interviewed for his job as an editorial writer at the *Sentinel* by Dunn who, according to Bowers, had been searching to find a substitute "to permit of his occasional meandering in the woods beside a stream with hook and line."[6]

In championing the Democratic party's interests, however, Dunn also managed to keep intact his strong belief in the power and advisability of honest government. When one

Democratic official wrote that the *Sentinel*, through Dunn's editorials, had been too hard on the party, Dunn responded in an editorial by lecturing his critic like a teacher correcting a wayward student:

> The worst enemy to any party is the man elected to office who violates the party pledges and brings on the party the disgrace and humiliation of obtaining goods under false pretenses. The betrayed party ought to be the first to demand his punishment. . . . The people are interested in good government more than in party success, and if a party wants success it must give the people good government. There is nothing to be gained by attempting to whitewash guilty or incompetent officials. The people are not fools. The democratic party in Indiana never prospered as it has since it inaugurated the policy of punishing its own rascals.[7]

The Democratic reformer had an opportunity to put the power of his convictions to the test following the presidential election of 1888, which pitted Indiana's own Benjamin Harrison as the GOP candidate against incumbent Democrat Grover Cleveland. The election, won by Harrison due in part to carrying his home state, still a key state in national elections, featured the usual corruption as each party scrambled to sway voters to its cause by using all means, both fair and foul. The motto of both major parties, *Century Magazine* said, seemed to be that "if we don't buy all the votes we can, our opponents will buy enough to carry the election, and that will never do. We must fight their corruption with greater corruption, because our own cause is so much purer and nobler and more patriotic than theirs."[8] These abuses, which had been accepted almost as a matter of course by Hoosiers in the past, were so flagrant that the public, and even politicians from both parties, demanded reform. Dunn took full advantage of his chance, he hoped, to once and for all cleanse the nineteenth state's squalid ballot box.

Voting in Indiana during the late nineteenth century usually involved a simple process. Under the state's election laws ballots were controlled and furnished to voters by political parties, and not to state officials. These "party ticket"

Benjamin Harrison

ballots, as they became known, contained the names of only a particular party's slate of candidates. The only state law regarding ballots required that they be printed on plain white paper three inches wide.[9] The practice of allowing political organizations to furnish ballots, a common one throughout the country in the 1880s, made it easy to bribe a class of voter known as a "floater," a person with no fixed party allegiance who sold his franchise to the highest bidder, be it Democrat or Republican. Party workers could buy these votes for as little as two dollars or as high as twenty dollars in tight elections.[10] These workers could ensure that once a floater was bought, he stayed bought, because, according to Eldon Cobb Evans's history of the Australian voting system in the United States, the workers were "permitted to have full view of the voter's ticket from the time it was given him until it was dropped in the ballot box."[11]

The number of floating votes in Indiana was estimated to have been ten thousand in the 1880 election and as high as twenty thousand in 1888.[12] Indiana University professor R. H. Dabney, in a letter to *The Nation*, went as far as to assert that the floating vote in Indiana during the 1888 election reached as high as thirty thousand. He told of one Bloomington resident who attempted to buy butter on election day but was told by a storekeeper that none was available—it had all been bought the day before to "butter sandwiches for floaters—for it would seem that even the Hoosier floater cannot live by free whiskey alone."[13]

Hoosier party workers went to unusual lengths to capture the floating vote. Thomas R. Marshall, Indiana governor and vice president, noted in his memoirs that it was not unusual "to corral what was known as the floating vote, fill it full of redeye, lock it up the night before election and march it to the polls early the next morning." A veteran poll watcher, Marshall knew of one Republican who planned to keep a floater in his room all night to guarantee that he voted the GOP ticket the next day. An enterprising Democrat, however, set fire to a nearby woodshed and cried out that the Republican's store was on fire. When the Republican ran off to make sure his business was safe, Marshall said, "the Democrats stole his chattel."[14]

Attempts by both parties to capture the floating vote played a key role in the 1888 presidential contest in Indiana. In spite of Benjamin Harrison's favorite son status, the state was up for grabs with both sides maneuvering desperately to win. The *Indianapolis Journal* reported in a 2 November 1888 editorial that it was the floating vote "that

The slogan "He's All Right" came from a popular campaign song in favor of Benjamin Harrison

IHS, C3054

the machinery and work of the contending parties are de-
signed to influence . . . and nobody but a ninny-hammer
would dream of anything else."[15] Walter Q. Gresham, who
had battled Harrison for the Republican presidential nomination, was informed by Chicago attorney Robert T. Lincoln
that W. H. H. Miller, Harrison's law partner, and Harrison's

William Wade Dudley

son, Russell, had visited Lincoln and asked for money to use for bribing Indiana voters. "The purchase of votes," Gresham wrote Noble Butler, "is carried on by both parties with little effort at concealment. If the thing goes on unchecked a catastrophe is inevitable. What is to become of us?"[16]

With Cleveland and Harrison running neck and neck, the Republican campaign in Indiana and throughout the country was rocked by the uncovering of the infamous "blocks of five" letter from William Wade Dudley, a Hoosier Civil War veteran who served as GOP national committee treasurer in the 1888 election. In the letter, which was sent to Indiana Republican county chairmen, Dudley warned that "only boodle and fraudulent votes and false counting of returns can beat us in the State [Indiana]." To counter this threat, he advised GOP workers to find out which Democrats at the polls were responsible for bribing voters and steer committed Democratic supporters to them, thereby exhausting the opposition's cash stockpile. "The result will fully justify the sacrifice of time and comfort," Dudley wrote, "and will be a source of satisfaction afterwards to those who help in this way. Lay great stress on this last matter. It will pay." The most damaging part of the letter, however, appeared in a sentence that became synonymous with political corruption. Dudley advised: "Divide the floaters into blocks of five, and put a trusted man with necessary funds in charge of these five, and make him responsible that none get away."[17]

GOP officials in Indiana took Dudley's counsel to heart. J. W. Jenks, who covered the 1888 presidential election for *Century Magazine*, reported that in one Hoosier county the chairman of the Republican committee discovered on the day before the election that his party and the Democrats had about the same amount of money available to use to influence voters at the polls, approximately two or three thousand dollars. Expecting a tight contest, the chairman leaked word to influential Republicans that the Democrats had raised six thousand dollars. Summoning three wealthy GOP members to a meeting, an additional three thousand dollars was collected. "The next day [election day] the Republicans were in position to offer $40 a vote at the opening of the polls," Jenks wrote. "By ten o'clock the Democratic money was gone, and after that the Republicans could buy votes at their own price."[18]

This political dynamite in Dudley's letter managed to find its way to the opposition camp, albeit with a little help. A Democratic mail clerk on the Ohio & Mississippi Railroad, suspicious about the large amount of mail being passed from GOP headquarters to Indiana Republicans, opened one of the letters, recognized its value to his party, and passed the damaging contents on to the Indiana Democratic State Central Committee chairman. The letter was printed in the *Indianapolis Sentinel* on 31 October 1888 under a banner headline reading "The Plot to Buy Indiana." Although an indignant Dudley and other top Republican officials declared that the letter was a forgery—and later claimed, correctly, that someone had been opening their mail—its contents received nationwide attention. Fanning the partisan flames even further, the *Sentinel* offered Dudley one thousand dollars if he would come to Indianapolis and swear that the letter published by the newspaper was a forgery; an offer Dudley never accepted.[19] The letter's revelations about political underhandedness, however, came too late to derail Harrison's campaign. The Hoosier Republican eked out a 2,300 vote plurality in Indiana. Cleveland won the nationwide popular vote, but Harrison handily captured the electoral college (233–168), and with that victory became president.[20]

After the election Harrison seemed blissfully unaware that political shenanigans might have played a role in his election. He told Sen. Matt Quay of Pennsylvania, GOP national chairman, that "Providence has given us the victory." Quay, a veteran politico who considered the new president a "political tenderfoot," was unmoved by Harrison's oratory. He later exclaimed to a Philadelphia journalist: "Think of the man! He ought to know that Providence hadn't a damned thing to do with it." The president, Quay said,

A slogan ball used by Benjamin Harrison supporters in the 1888 presidential election. A similar ball had been used in William Henry Harrison's 1840 presidential campaign

might "never learn how close a number of men were compelled to approach the gates of the penitentiary to make him President."[21]

Meanwhile, the aftershock from Dudley's letter reverberated throughout the Hoosier State. Dunn, at that time in charge of literary work for the Democratic State Central Committee and temporarily serving as *Sentinel* editor, saw the continued furor about the Dudley letter as an opportunity to revamp Indiana's voting method. "I had long been disgusted with corruption in politics," Dunn said, "and the knowledge that the state had been bought by the Republicans roused a determination to try for reform." To remedy matters, he proposed to put the full weight of the *Sentinel* behind establishing a secret ballot based on a method first developed in Australia in the 1850s.[22]

The Australian ballot system (also known as the "official" ballot), which was passed into law in that country in 1857–58, was a relatively new and novel way for Americans to vote. The first secret ballot law in the United States had been adopted for the city of Louisville, Kentucky, just nine months prior to the 1888 election. Massachusetts became the first state to approve the system shortly after Louisville enacted its law. The Australian voting method was easy to understand; the government became responsible for printing and distributing ballots to voters, and each polling place had to provide a way for voters to mark their ballots in secret. Reformers argued that this method of exercising suffrage would help eliminate vote buying "by removing the knowledge of whether it had been successful."[23]

In hopes of seeing the Australian system become law in Indiana, Dunn, as part of his campaign on behalf of the new voting method, called on Lafayette P. Custer, an Indianapolis labor leader and telegraph operator, and, according to Dunn, the only man he could find in the entire city of Indianapolis able to write intelligently on the election reform issue. In an article for the *Sentinel*, Custer outlined the six main features of the Australian system: printing and distributing the ballots at public expense; enabling a voter to mark his ballot in secrecy; regulating the methods used to

select candidates; defining bribery; defining "undue influence" upon voters; and limiting the amount a candidate
could spend on an election. The floating vote, Custer predicted, would continue to increase each year under the present ballot system in Indiana since it allowed "the landlord,
money lord and corporate wealth generally to levy tribute
on the masses." If some way was not found to limit the influence of political managers, Custer continued, "we might
as well call free government a farce." Noting those critics
who argued that bribery could still exist even under the
Australian system, the labor leader answered them by
pointing out that "the briber would not trust a voter who
would be guilty of selling his vote. . . . A man could sell his
vote to a dozen men if buyers could be found and after all
vote his own sentiments and no one be the wiser."[24]

Custer's article, with Dunn's editorial endorsement, appeared in the *Sentinel* on 19 November 1888. The Democratic newspaper continued to beat the drum on behalf of
election reform as the 1889 Indiana legislative session
neared. The reform effort had an immediate impact. In a
manner that foreshadowed his work on a new Indiana constitution in 1911, Dunn placed his imprint on the Australian ballot issue. After a meeting with outgoing Democratic governor Isaac P. Gray, and subsequent sessions that
included input from several legislators, the historian wrote
an Australian ballot bill for consideration by the General
Assembly.[25]

Dunn's attempt at election reform benefited from the simple fact that the 1889 legislature was dominated by one
party: the Democrats controlled both the House and Senate.
But even newly elected Republican governor Alvin P. Hovey
called for action to transform the state's corrupt election voting process. In his inaugural address to the lawmakers on
14 January 1889, Hovey admitted that the ballot in Indiana, and in many other states, had been debased. He leveled blame at both political parties, noting that the situation was so bad that "in the eyes of many respectable men,
it [bribing voters] seems to be no longer regarded as a
crime." The governor recommended to the legislators that

the state's election laws be revised and offered a proposal whereby every elected official would be required in his oath of office to swear that he had "not directly or indirectly given, promised, advanced, or paid any money, or given or conveyed any other article of value to any person or persons to aid, assist, or procure his election or appointment."[26]

Even with the GOP governor's plea for reform, and his editorials for the *Sentinel*, Dunn had trouble convincing his fellow Democrats to support a measure to revise the existing voting system. He recalled that one longtime party official "insisted to the last that he preferred the old system, 'so that he could take a floater back of the schoolhouse, and mark his ticket for him.'" Dunn, however, continued to hammer away in the *Sentinel* on the absolute need for the Democrats to secure ballot reform. "The legislature now in session will . . . destroy every reasonable chance of democratic success in this state for years to come, if it fails to pass a law which will insure a free and honest ballot," Dunn wrote.[27]

Honest elections were essential for the Democratic party, he argued, because that party could not compete successfully with the GOP's "election rascality" since the Democrats, because of their support for tariff reduction, faced continuous opposition from "the capitalist element . . . and it [business] furnished the funds [to the GOP] for vote-buying."[28] He also charged that with the Republican control of the federal court system through their party's patronage power, court officials were more inclined to "punish Democratic scoundrels and release Republican scoundrels."[29] With those facts in mind, Dunn reasoned that the best hope for Democratic success at the polls was to have "intelligent and honest voters, and not . . . ignorant and corrupt ones." For the Democratic party to flourish, he continued, "honesty is the best policy from political as well as other considerations."[30]

What emerged from the General Assembly was the second secret ballot law to be passed by a state and one that became a model that other states followed. Commenting on the law, Dunn noted that it was a modified version of a proposal originally made by a New York reform organization. One merit of Indiana's version, according to Dunn, was that each party could check on the activities of the other, as Democrats and Republicans had equal representation on election boards. Under the new system the state, not the political parties, furnished the ballots for use on election day. Unlike other versions of the Australian system, however, the Hoosier law reflected the strong party loyalties in the state by featuring a "party-column" ballot, which listed the nominees with their political party affiliations, giving voters the opportunity to mark a straight-ticket vote. Reform, in the case of the Australian ballot, was "tempered by the political culture environment of Indiana," and changed enough to meet "prevailing political circumstances."[31]

Unlike Dunn, who commingled his reform and political party activities throughout his career, purist reformers were appalled by Indiana's partisan alteration of the Australian ballot. Although the ballots were now controlled by the state government, political parties received both official recognition and ballot placement because any candidates placed on the ticket had to receive certification by the party hierarchy.[32] Dunn himself noted that while he was crafting the new election law he had modified legislation from other areas of the country "to meet our established customs as far as possible"—a custom that included hearty and vibrant political parties.[33]

Instituting the modified Australian ballot system in Indiana—and in the thirty-seven other states that passed some form of the Australian method by 1892—failed to stop completely corruption at the ballot box, a fact its proponents freely admitted. It did, however, provide an essential initial step in helping secure honest elections for Indiana and other states. In a 2 January 1890 editorial the *Indianapolis News* lavished praise on the Democrats for what it called a "magnificent reform." Referring to the Hoosier State's previous reputation for notoriously corrupt elections, the *News* said that "nothing of late years has done more for the State's good name than the fact of this law."[34] Voters could now make their election choices in private, eliminating, as one scholar described it, the "intimidating party aura" that had existed under the old voting system.[35] The *Sentinel* proudly proclaimed that by passing the new election law Democrats in the legislature, who lined up solidly behind the measure, would see it stand as "a lasting monument to their integrity, their wisdom and their patriotism." The Democratic party organ later loftily stated that the election law was "the most important measure ever enacted by an Indiana legislature."[36]

To Dunn's way of thinking, however, the Australian ballot system constituted an incomplete reform. Along with the new voting arrangement, the legislature had passed a bribery law that Dunn claimed made the 1890, 1892, and 1894 elections "the cleanest that had been known in Indiana for years." The bribery law's effectiveness was emasculated by subsequent Republican legislation, according to Dunn. Consequently, although the Australian system secured orderly elections with diminished chances for voter intimidation, Dunn believed it fell short of eliminating vote buying outright. What was needed, Dunn argued, were voting laws "based on educational qualification, and all suffrage conditioned on payment of taxes."[37]

Dunn's hope for continued improvement of Indiana's ballot—and success for the Democratic party—endured a long fallow period. With the end of Claude Matthews's term in 1897, twelve years passed before a Democrat again sat in the governor's chair. In 1909, however, the Democrats' days of wandering in the political wilderness ended as a man Dunn termed the "ablest Democratic governor" since Thomas Hendricks took over the office.[38] In Thomas Riley Marshall, Dunn found a Democratic politician willing to join him in his quest to secure an honest and intelligent electorate. Before continuing that crusade, however, Dunn became involved in a reform effort that took root in Indianapolis's muddy streets—a new city charter.

4

Dunn and the 1891 Indianapolis City Charter

INDIANAPOLIS IN THE LAST HALF OF THE NINETEENTH CENTURY was a bustling, thriving city. Just seventy years after commissioners appointed by the Indiana General Assembly convened at John McCormick's tavern and agreed on a site for a new state capital at the confluence of the West Fork of the White River and Fall Creek, the population of the city had surpassed one hundred thousand—a growth rate surpassing even that of Los Angeles's first seventy years.[1] For entertainment, citizens took the streetcar to Fairview Park, located northwest of the city, or were treated to performances by such great names as the Barrymores, Lilly Langtry, and Sarah Bernhardt at the English Opera House or the Park Theater. For refreshment before or after a performance, residents of the Circle City could visit numerous German beer gardens and saloons. Business and industry also prospered. The *Indianapolis Herald* reported that in 1888 the city contained 892 factories producing an annual product of $49,000,000 and supported 1,416 retail stores and 398 wholesale houses.[2]

Beneath the feet of busy Indianapolis pedestrians lurked a problem; the streets used for travel and commerce were often in appalling condition. The level surface and rich soil that had attracted the state commissioners to pick Indianapolis as the site for the new capital were perfect for agricultural purposes, noted Dunn, but they "were serious drawbacks in the drainage and street construction of a city." Streets were generally paved with boulders or cobblestones, which created a bumpy ride for vehicles and dangers for pedestrians. The uneven surface collected water and other, more foul, substances deposited by horse-drawn wagons and carriages that often splashed unsuspecting passersby.[3]

A few attempts were made by the city government to improve the quality of Indianapolis's roadways, but most of the changes were hardly better than what had existed before. Cedar blocks were used to pave Meridian Street between New York and Seventh (now Sixteenth) Streets in 1882, but the blocks soon fell into disrepair. Six years later the city tried again. Washington Street from Mississippi (now Senate Avenue) to Alabama Streets was paved with a patented material called Vulcanite at a cost of $74,488.68. A satisfactory enough surface in cold weather, the paving turned into the consistency of chewing gum in hot weather, causing Indianapolis citizens to nickname it "the Yucatan pavement." Exacerbating the problem was competition between two Indianapolis gas companies in 1890 to be the first to have their gas mains installed. The companies tore up the city's streets, Dunn said, and created in their wake "miniature mountain ranges along most of the streets, cutting off drainage and impeding passage."[4]

Indianapolis street scene, circa 1890s

Although failures, Dunn noted that these efforts were helpful in that they educated "intelligent people to the importance of some adequate authority to take charge of public improvements." The 1889 Indiana General Assembly took the first step toward solving the problem by passing a bill establishing a Board of Public Works for Indianapolis. This "excellent measure," said Dunn, had only one problem. The bill provided that members of the first board would be elected by the General Assembly (Democratic in this instance), and their successors would be appointed by the Indianapolis mayor (a Republican at the time). Republican mayor Caleb Denny refused to approve the bonds of both the members of this first Board of Public Works and those of a police and fire department board also approved by the legislature. According to Dunn, "This left matters, at the close of 1889, where they were at the beginning."[5]

Two actions, however, helped pave the way for improvement of Indianapolis's streets. At the 1889 session of the General Assembly, Sen. James M. Barrett of Allen County, who also engineered the passage of the Australian ballot reform measure through the legislature, introduced a measure that made it easier for property owners to pay for improvements over a ten-year period through the issuance of bonds. The Barrett Law, as it became known, not only promoted public improvements in Indiana's cities and towns but also was used as a model in other states. In Indianapolis alone from 1890 to 1909 a total of $5,546,061.89 in Barrett Law bonds was issued. According to Dunn, the new law "reconciled hundreds of men to the policy of public improvements on an extensive scale—a scale that would have created intolerable burdens if the expense had been obliged to be met in full on the completion of the work, as it was before."[6]

The second step to enhancing the capital city's roadways, and revising the way in which the city was governed, came in 1890 with the creation of the Commercial Club, the forerunner of today's Indianapolis Chamber of Commerce. The brainchild of *Indianapolis News* reporter William Fortune and pharmaceutical entrepreneur Col.

Colonel Eli Lilly

Eli Lilly, the Commercial Club was organized in February 1890 "to promote the commercial and manufacturing interests and the general welfare of Indianapolis and vicinity." The organization immediately set out to heighten the public's awareness of the need to improve the city's avenues by sponsoring a Street Paving Exposition in April at Tomlinson Hall where paving companies from throughout the country exhibited their wares. Approximately twelve thousand people attended the four-day exposition, the first of its kind in the nation.[7]

Changing the character of Indianapolis's streets, however, was dependent upon revising another aspect of the city—its government. Indianapolis, like many growing urban centers during the late nineteenth and early twentieth centuries, discovered that it required a "more effective, positive city administration that could tackle community affairs and draw for support upon a sense of common concern for mutual problems," noted Samuel P. Hays in his study of the American urban scene from 1885 to 1914. Business leaders and reformers across the country, Hays argues, worked together to establish in city governments "clearer lines of authority and to increase the mayor's power to appoint his subordinates and to initiate policy."[8] Large cities throughout the country in the 1880s—Brooklyn, Boston, Philadelphia—had reorganized their governments under new city charters that gave their mayors increased authority, hoping to institute honesty and efficiency in local government.[9] To accomplish this task in Indianapolis, the Commercial Club and its allies, which included Dunn, set about to alter the antiquated Indianapolis city charter.

The Charter of 1853, passed by the General Assembly following the adoption of the 1851 Indiana Constitution and which applied to all cities with populations of three thousand or more, placed control of the municipality in the hands of the city council. The council had the power to levy taxes, annex property, appoint city officials, and pass ordinances for governing the city. Under this system the mayor enjoyed little authority, serving merely as the president of the board of councilmen and as police court judge.

On 10 March 1890 the Commercial Club sponsored a meeting at the Indianapolis Board of Trade Hall devoted to the city charter. At that meeting a resolution was passed calling on the Commercial Club's board of directors to appoint a committee to "consider the matter of revising the laws governing the city, the formulation of new laws believed to be needed, and the embodiment of the same in a bill covering the entire subject of city government." The next day the club's board selected as members of the committee Augustus L. Mason, a local attorney; Samuel E. Morss, *Indianapolis Sentinel* publisher; and Granville S. Wright, a city alderman. Joining these prominent men on the panel were Mayor Thomas L. Sullivan, Board of Aldermen president Isaac J. Thalman, and City Council Finance Committee chairman William Wesley Woollen. Dunn noted that the committee had been organized on a nonpartisan basis, with Morss and Sullivan keeping the Democratic party abreast of developments, while Thalman and Wright did the same for the GOP.[10]

The committee met in an office located at 90½ East Market Street throughout the summer of 1890 with "tireless regularity," said Dunn, and without the use of "stimulants." After they had finished their work for the evening, he noted, the committee members refreshed themselves not with alcoholic beverages, but with soft drinks. In preparing a new city charter the committee used as a model two basic examples: Philadelphia's Bullitt Law, which authorized the mayor to appoint a board of public works and other officers, and the city charter of Brooklyn, which was constructed on the federal plan with a division of government into legislative, judicial, and executive branches.[11]

After ten months of effort, the committee issued a new city charter the main feature of which, according to Dunn, was the "entire separation of the executive, legislative and judicial functions, all administrative functions being transferred to the executive department." Most of the power of city government now lay in the hands of the mayor. Under the new charter the person in that office appointed the Board of Public Works, the Board of Public Safety, the Board of Health, and the city engineer. These appointments did not have to be approved by the twenty-five-member city council and five-member board of aldermen provided for in the charter, and the mayor could, at any time, remove from office those he appointed. "The mayor," said Dunn, "is really made the key-stone of the arch." This fact made it doubly important for the people to, as Dunn put it, "select the very best material in electing a mayor." Because the new charter lodged great power in city officials, he warned voters that Indianapolis's welfare depended "chiefly on the character of the officials selected"—an admonition that would come back to haunt Dunn later during his second stint as city controller.[12]

Introduced before the Indiana General Assembly on 9 January 1891 as House Bill No. 44, the new city charter for Indianapolis seemed assured of smooth sailing, as Democrats controlled both the House (74–26) and Senate (34–16). The measure as written, however, received a less than enthusiastic response from some members of the Marion County delegation in the General Assembly. At a meeting involving the Commercial Club committee, Indianapolis lawmakers, and other interested citizens (including Dunn) held at the statehouse on 22 January, Gen. John Coburn, a former congressman and prominent local attorney, denigrated the bill as providing for "an absolute monarchy for the city of Indianapolis—the Mayor electing the sub-officers, and not the people. I have not had an opportunity to carefully study it, but tonight, after coming into this room, I read some of its provisions, and I was amazed." After Coburn had finished his remarks, William P. Fishback, who had spoken in favor of the new charter, turned to Dunn and whispered, "Just wait and see Gus skin him." Augustus L. (Gus) Mason did just that. "The General's theory of local self-government is a good one," acknowledged Mason, but it did not apply in this case because of his "ignorance of the bill in question" and "his absolute misstatements" regarding its provisions. Coburn later called Mason's remarks "beneath my contempt."[13]

Although Dunn had intended to attend the meeting only as an "innocent bystander," the reformer, once engaged, had to offer his suggestions on the matter. When asked for his opinion, Dunn said that he favored the measure but, because of the possibility of gerrymandering, he urged that the Board of Aldermen be eliminated and instead that the measure should include "enough councilmen-at-large to off-set any possible gerrymander advantage." Also, Dunn noted that the Board of Public Works had "unrestricted power in the matter of street improvement." With this in mind, he suggested that if a majority of property owners on a street "did not want a proposed improvement they should have the right of remonstrance."[14]

Both of Dunn's ideas influenced the final version of the bill (in which the Board of Aldermen was eliminated), but his greatest contribution to the cause of the new Indianapolis charter arose from his political connections and his willingness to put aside partisan issues in favor of real reform for the city's government. During the debate on the new city charter, Dunn was serving as state librarian and writing for the *Indianapolis Sentinel*. Utilizing the same detective skills that served him so well as a historian, he discovered that several people whom Morss trusted regarding the legislation were in fact ready to betray him. These people, members of Dunn's own party, had adopted the plan, according to Dunn in his history of Indianapolis, of allowing the charter to go through but of amending it by making the Board of Public Works elective from three districts, one from the city north of Ohio Street and the other two south, divided by a north and south line. "It was supposed that this would insure two Democratic members, and the board of works was considered the one important thing in the whole system," Dunn said.[15]

Forewarned, Morss prepared a "scorching editorial" denouncing the attempted subversion of the charter. The plans of this group, Morss wrote, fell under the "limits of what is commonly known as 'practical politics.' In other words, they desire to have the charter so amended as to give an unfair advantage to the democratic party in this city." Reiterating the newspaper's position that "practical politics is not good politics," Morss noted that if the attempt to revise the charter in this underhanded way succeeded, it spelled doom for the Democratic party at the next city election. "We know the temper of the people of Indianapolis," Morss wrote in his editorial. "They are tired of this political pettifogging in city affairs. They want the city's business transacted on business principles. The party that honestly endeavors to do this will receive their support, but they will never ratify any such piece of political trickery as this." The *Sentinel* publisher expressed his astonishment that men "who profess to have political sagacity should advocate so foolish a move."[16]

Revulsion over the plot even prompted the *Indianapolis News* to jump on the bandwagon and urge that the new charter be passed. "As a whole we believe the scheme to be the soundest and best that has ever been devised, and an imperative requisite for the good career and fair progress of Indianapolis," the *News* proclaimed. Along with bringing more supporters into the fray, Dunn said that exposing the plot stopped the "double-dealing with the *Sentinel*," leaving the friends of the charter with "an open field, and their enemies all in front of them."[17]

The new charter made its way through the Indiana House with only minor amendments, passing by a vote of 65 to 13 on 16 February 1891. The measure faced a tougher battle, however, in the Senate, where it encountered, said Dunn, the one man in the General Assembly who opposed the measure "as a matter of disinterested principle"—Frank B. Burke, a Democrat from Clark County. The pragmatic Dunn grudgingly respected Burke for being a "brilliant genius," but claimed that the lawmaker's devotion to principle disqualified him from important legislative work "in which abstract principles, in their logical extremes, have usually to be abandoned, for the simple reason that human beings do not live on a logical basis." Dunn partially agreed with the theory that great legislation was the product of compromise, but "only so far as the compromise is in the line of adapting it to actual human conditions, as against theories." In the case of the new city charter for Indianapolis, Burke opposed a section that authorized the Board of Public Works to purchase or build and operate water and electric utilities. "He [Burke] felt that true Democratic principles called for a vote of the people on such important matters," said Dunn.[18]

The charter bill also faced some last-minute attempts at revision in the Senate's committee on the affairs of Indianapolis. On 28 February 1891 the committee approved a majority report signed by William Clinton Thompson, a Marion County Democrat, that, according to the *Sentinel*, made "such radical changes that there is little left of the original bill." Some of the alterations to the bill included giving the city council the power to fix the districts from which members of the Board of Public Works were to be appointed, requiring a two-thirds vote from the council before the mayor could remove a city official, and disallowing the council from making an improvement on a street if a majority of property owners along the line of the street remonstrate against it in writing. A minority report, signed by Republican senators Orrin Hubbell of Elkhart County and John Yaryan of Wayne County, made only minor changes to the bill.[19]

Unwilling to see the bill emasculated, all the members of the citizens committee that had originally prepared the charter quickly issued a statement addressed to the citizens of Indianapolis. The statement, printed just a few days after the Senate committee's action, said the following:

> In our opinion the changes proposed absolutely subvert and destroy all sound principles of municipal government. The city of Indianapolis feels deeply the need of municipal reform. Its enemies should not be permitted to defeat the proposed charter directly, nor to pervert it by amendments which deprive it of every element of reform.
>
> In behalf of ourselves, and of the organizations by which we were appointed, we repudiate the charter as a whole, if the amendments proposed by the majority report of the senate committee are adopted. We believe that any law which fails to completely separate the legislative, executive and judicial functions of government is unwise. We heartily approve the report submitted by the minority of the senate committee.[20]

The committee won its fight; on 3 March 1891 the full Senate substituted the committee's minority report for the majority report. Sen. Timothy Edward Howard, a Democrat representing St. Joseph and Starke Counties, championed the minority report during the Senate debate. "Complaints are coming up from all the populous cities of the evil effects of bad government and from Indianapolis particularly," Howard said. "We have it in our power to remedy this evil and should not hesitate to do so." He concluded by claiming that if the majority report was adopted, the people of Indianapolis "may expect no better government than they have now."

Speaking on behalf of the majority report, Sen. Cortez Ewing, a Democrat representing Decatur and Shelby Counties, argued that under the provisions of the new charter the mayor of Indianapolis "becomes a 'czar,' and to a limited extent clothed with all the power of the czar of Russia." And, since the mayor had the power to appoint the Board of Public Works, that body would become in effect vice czars. "That's the important question in controversy. That's what the majority report seeks to prevent," said Ewing. "Why Boss Tweed never operated under a charter so free."[21]

Ewing's warnings fell on deaf ears as the Senate, by a 42 to 3 vote on 3 March 1891, passed the charter bill substantially as it was written. The measure was signed into law by Republican governor Alvin P. Hovey three days later.[22] Praising the General Assembly for its action, the *Sentinel* editorialized that the legislature had rendered the same "service to the people of Indianapolis that the last legislature rendered to the people of Indiana when it established the Australian election system." The *Sentinel* also patted itself, and other daily newspapers in Indianapolis, on the back for their efforts on the charter's behalf. "The newspapers largely created the healthy public sentiment which proved so potential with the legislature as to bear down the powerful interests which were arrayed against the charter," the *Sentinel* said. The charter's success, the editorial went on to say, showed what could be done when the power of the press and an "aroused and organized public opinion" joined forces.[23]

Through his support for giving the mayor enormous authority for Indianapolis's government, however, Dunn sowed the seeds for his own political humiliation twenty-five years later. Appointed city controller by Democratic mayor Joseph E. Bell in 1914, Dunn, after two years in office, came under

A Gaar Williams cartoon, titled "The Mustacheless Stranger," of Dunn as city controller that appeared in the *Indianapolis News*

fire from the *Indianapolis News* for his practice of using interest earned on contractors' guaranty bonds for personal gain. According to the *News*, in the spring of 1914 the Board of Public Works ruled that checks submitted from the lowest bidder for municipal improvements should be deposited with the city controller instead of sitting uncashed in the board's office until contracts were let. Although the certified checks from failed bidders on city contracts often were held by the clerk of the Board of Public Works, the newspaper alleged that sometimes a number of certified checks on the same contract would be turned over to Dunn's office.

Dunn admitted to the *News* that he cashed such certified checks and drew "interest on such money held by him as 'trustee' until the time came to settle with the contractors." Because the income from this source was very regular, the newspaper charged that Dunn probably had "considerable money from this source on hand at all times." Although there was no law prohibiting such a practice, and previous occupants of the office had also followed this custom, Mayor Bell ordered Dunn in December 1915 to cease collecting interest for his personal use. Records indicate that Dunn's office received $178,947 in certified checks in 1914 and $181,915 in certified checks in 1915.[24]

Six months after the *News*'s exposé, Mayor Bell asked for and received Dunn's resignation, along with those of John Reddington, deputy city controller, and John Pugh, deputy auditor of the Board of School Commissioners. His action, the mayor claimed, was on "account of the general condition that has existed in connection with his management of the office. The business of his office has been so conducted that much criticism has come to me concerning the management thereof." Although one of the reasons cited by Bell for Dunn's dismissal was the controller's practice of collecting interest for personal use, the *News* reported that Dunn was being made the scapegoat for irregularities conducted by political appointees. The newspaper noted that "it is a well-known fact that Dunn never appointed any of his assistants but that they were chosen by the mayor." Reddington, Pugh, and John Shaughnessy, a former bookkeeper in the controller's office, were indicted by a Marion County grand jury.[25]

It was, in fact, Dunn who first exposed the irregularities in his office when he had Shaughnessy arrested for forging the name of a local contractor, George W. McCrary, to a check made payable by the city controller to McCrary for $119.25. Later, Reddington and Pugh were charged with improperly collecting vehicle license fees between 1 July and 31 December 1915, turning over to the city only half of the fees charged. In an editorial titled "Dunn the Goat," the *News* noted it was commonly believed that the "incompetent party men whom the controller employed were thrust upon him, and that the 'higher-ups' are as much, if not more, to blame for the loose methods which the mayor now so heroically denounces and which have long prevailed in the controller's office." Still, the editorial indicated the newspaper and community would have had more sympathy for Dunn if he had "taken the initiative and cleaned out the political stables himself."[26]

Ever faithful to the party he supported throughout his life, Dunn refused to place the blame for his troubles on Bell, who had the power to kick the controller out of office because of the 1890–91 city charter Dunn helped to institute. Asked by an *Indianapolis Star* reporter if he planned to resign without any ceremony, Dunn replied: "Why, of course I will." After the swearing in of his successor, Reginald H. Sullivan (later mayor of Indianapolis), Dunn, as he left the controller's office for the last time, stopped long enough to issue the comment that he had "done nothing to apologize for and a man would be a fool in a case like this to talk about the rest of it."[27]

In this matter Dunn had allowed his party spirit to overcome his zeal for reform. As the *Indianapolis News* pointed out, Dunn had been induced by the Democratic party to "commit himself to the defense of situations which, as a searcher after truth in his books, he hardly would have defended."[28] But three years before he became city controller, the Hoosier historian had used the Democratic party, especially its standard-bearer in Indiana, Gov. Thomas R. Marshall, to further what Dunn believed was a key to good government in the state: furnishing an honest electorate through a new Indiana constitution.

5

Dunn, Governor Thomas R. Marshall, and the Indiana Constitution

AT THE OPENING OF THE INDIANA GENERAL ASSEMBLY'S SIXTY-seventh session on 5 January 1911, Gov. Thomas R. Marshall, a Democrat, addressed a legislature different from the one he had appeared before two years earlier following his gubernatorial victory over Republican opponent James E. Watson. At that time power had been split between Democrats who controlled the House and Republicans who held a majority in the Senate. Democratic gains in the 1910 election, however, gave that party majorities in both chambers for the 1911 session. Despite this partisan advantage Marshall's message to the lawmakers lent credence to his designation by many observers as a "Progressive with the brakes on."[1] He called on the General Assembly to act on such issues as compulsory workmen's compensation, new child labor laws, and voter registration reform. Early in his speech the governor also noted that there were "certain provisions of our constitution which do not meet present conditions." Although he did not wish to see the document "radically altered," the sixty-year-old constitution was in need of some revisions, which would, among other things, curtail aliens' voting rights, increase the length of legislative sessions, and ease the often complicated constitutional amendment process.[2]

Marshall softened his call for changes to the 1851 Constitution by conceding to the legislators that there were "other important matters pending before you." Should these other matters be decided, Marshall continued, "it is not improbable that I shall again address you upon them

Indiana State Library

Indiana governor Thomas R. Marshall

[the constitution revisions]."[3] The governor's offhand mention of possible changes in the constitution was a poor indication of the legislative firestorm he would soon ignite. In a little over a month's time the General Assembly was in full partisan cry when it was presented with not just a few amendments or a call for a full-fledged constitutional convention, but rather an entirely new Indiana constitution. Republican opponents blasted Marshall's action, terming it illegal and a usurpation of authority on the governor's part. If allowed to pass, warned Republican representative Jesse E. Eschbach, the measure could "lead to internal strife and dissension and eventually to revolution."[4]

The document that caused such bitter partisan bickering became known as the "Tom Marshall Constitution." Such a designation was misleading, however, since it had not been created after consultation by the governor with his usual friends and advisers, nor in the usual give-and-take of the legislative process. Instead, as Marshall's biographer Charles M. Thomas wrote years later, work on the new Indiana constitution "had been done quietly in the Governor's office." According to Thomas, the governor was "largely influenced by the advice of one man whom he relied upon to draft much of the constitution."[5] That one man was Dunn, who wrote the revised constitution and suggested a way around the cumbersome constitutional amendment process in Indiana by bypassing the usual reform methods for the more radical approach of introducing the new document to the lawmakers. Once it passed the legislature it would be presented to Hoosier voters for ratification at the 1912 election and, if successful, would become law.

Dunn had pinned his chance for the betterment of Indiana's ballot, to his mind the key feature of the new constitution, on Marshall's coattails. Since the passage of the Australian ballot law in 1889, Dunn had seen that law continually weakened; he yearned for a chance to once again put matters right. He discovered a willing partner in the governor, a Columbia City lawyer who was one of the unlikeliest candidates ever for Indiana's highest office.

Although he had been involved in Democratic party activities for most of his life, and had even formed a Democratic Club while a student at Wabash College, Marshall's only experience in seeking office had been a failed bid for prosecuting attorney. After losing that race, Marshall returned to his law practice and continued to be active in party affairs. He served two years as the Twelfth District

Democratic Committee chairman and was asked to run for Congress in 1906, an honor he declined. When asked if he might someday consider another campaign for elective office, Marshall said he doubted he ever would again, unless that race happened to be for governor.[6]

The "Marshall for Governor" bandwagon started rolling in earnest in the early fall of 1907. While Marshall and his wife were on vacation in northern Michigan, longtime Indiana newspaper reporter and Washington correspondent Louis Ludlow, Marshall's friend, became the first journalist to put forward the Columbia City lawyer's name as a gubernatorial candidate. Ludlow's suggestion was immediately picked up by newspapers throughout northern Indiana. In addition to this editorial support, delegates to the Democratic state convention from the Twelfth District pledged their votes on Marshall's behalf.[7]

The Democratic state convention held 25 March 1908 at Tomlinson Hall in Indianapolis displayed a party in disarray. Forces loyal to longtime Democratic boss Thomas Taggart lined up in support of his handpicked gubernatorial candidate, Samuel M. Ralston, who would eventually succeed Marshall as governor. Meanwhile, those opposing Taggart's control of the party touted the candidacy of state senator L. Ert Slack. Commenting on the intraparty divisions, Marshall noted that it was a "difficult thing to find a man who was a Democrat—just a plain, unadorned, undiluted, unterrified Democrat." With the convention deadlocked after four ballots, Ralston—pressed to do so by his patron Taggart—announced his withdrawal from the race. With Ralston's departure, voters quickly switched to Marshall, and he received his party's nomination for governor on the subsequent ballot. The dark horse, as Marshall put it, had transformed himself "from His Accidency to His Excellency."[8]

With the Democratic party firmly united behind his candidacy, Marshall turned his efforts to convincing Hoosier voters that he was the best man for the job. He conducted a low-key campaign, telling the crowds that gathered to hear him speak he was the "candidate of no faction and candidate of no interest; that I had no strings to me; no promises out; owed nobody anything except good will; that I had a perfectly good [law] practise at home; did not care whether I was elected or not; but if they were in accord with Democratic principles I was soliciting their votes for the party and not for myself." Marshall even claimed to have returned more than $7,000 in campaign funds he received in the mail. Instead of using those funds, he borrowed $3,750 from Columbia City's First National Bank to finance his campaign for governor, an amount he repaid only after finishing his two subsequent terms as vice president under Woodrow Wilson.[9]

While Marshall's understated campaign style proved to be effective with Hoosiers, Cong. James E. Watson, the Republican gubernatorial nominee, experienced difficulties within his own party. Gov. J. Frank Hanly, a tireless advocate of temperance, had prodded the Republican party into including in its platform a plank calling for a county option law on the liquor question. With this pledge on the books, Hanly went one step farther. Three weeks before the election he called a special session of the General Assembly that ultimately passed the county option measure. (Democrats had favored using the city, township, or ward as the basis to decide the question of whether or not liquor should be allowed in an area.)

The Democratic candidate fiercely opposed Hanly's use of executive power. Speaking in Rockport before the special session got under way, Marshall unwittingly foreshadowed attacks that later would be leveled against him in his attempt at constitutional reform when he compared Hanly to a dictator giving orders with no thought as to what the people might really want. Such actions, said Marshall, were a "violation of constitutional government, for under a constitutional government the people themselves rule."[10]

Watson also disputed the wisdom of Hanly's legislative posturing, but he had a more personal stake in the matter. He blamed Hanly's insistence on obtaining passage of the county option law before the campaign's finish as a major reason why he would go on to lose the governor's race to

Marshall poses with Republican senator Albert J. Beveridge, who, in 1912, ran for Indiana governor on the Progressive party ticket and lost to Democrat Samuel M. Ralston

Marshall. "When this was done," Watson insisted in his memoirs, "it took my platform squarely out from under me and thus relieved any Democrats who believed in county local option from the necessity of voting for me to get what they wanted." The Republican congressman acknowledged that opposition from organized labor also played a role in his approximately fifteen thousand-vote defeat.[11]

Indiana governor during a time in American history when Progressives across the country were advocating such liberal governmental changes as the initiative, referendum, and recall, along with other measures to combat society's problems, Marshall nevertheless proved to be a cautious reformer. He advocated clear and equal separation of powers among the legislative, executive, and judicial branches of government. The governor's wary approach to reform was highlighted in his opening message to the General Assembly on 11 January 1909 in which he counseled the lawmakers to be cautious in enacting any new laws. "Undigested legislation," Marshall warned, "must inevitably result in evil to the body politic. Your record will be made not by the amount but by the character of the work you do."[12] The divided General Assembly (Democrats controlled the House and Republicans the Senate) took Marshall's advice to heart. Although the governor had asked them to consider such reform measures as the direct election of United States senators, improved railroad and insurance company legislation, and the creation of a State Board of Accounts, only the last of these was enacted.

Paradoxically, some Indiana historians have proposed the belief that the state's greatest attempt at reform came not during the Progressive Era but in the late 1890s. Dunn was one of the first to champion this interpretation, noting that the legislature of 1889 "adopted more and better laws than any legislature that preceded or followed it; but what was of more importance, it set a pace for its successors."[13] A more recent assessment agrees that the reforms pursued in later years, especially during the period from 1912 to 1916, "merely modelled themselves on the precedents set in 1889."[14] This is true of Dunn's efforts on behalf of a new state constitution, which he saw as a continuation of his work to purify Hoosier elections.

As disappointed as Marshall was with the legislative setbacks he suffered during the 1909 session, he seemed determined to keep the lines of authority among the different branches of government clear. Speaking before fellow Democrats at the party's 1910 convention, he cautioned his audience about the dangers of one-man government. Even though such a government might sometimes produce good laws, "in so doing, it will establish a precedent whereby an evil-minded man may work intolerable wrong and overthrow our system."[15] Marshall believed that the state's chief executive should not use "his power, his prestige and his right of appointment to overawe or coerce the legislative department of government."[16]

On one issue, however, Marshall swept aside his usual political beliefs in favor of the same domineering methods for which he had condemned his predecessor during the gubernatorial campaign. The issue subjecting Marshall to an eventual avalanche of condemnation from Republicans was one that had bedeviled the state for a number of years: reform of the 1851 Indiana Constitution. The General Assembly had long debated ways to amend what had become an outdated document and met with repeated failures due to a complicated process for effecting constitutional revisions. According to terms outlined in the 1851 Constitution, any amendment had to be passed by two consecutive legislative sessions before it could be considered by Hoosier voters.

The cumbersome amendment process was highlighted in the early 1900s when a lawyers' group attempted to revise a constitutional provision that admitted to the bar applicants whose only qualification consisted of possessing a good moral character. A bill authorizing the General Assembly to set stricter qualifications for admission to the bar successfully passed two consecutive legislative sessions (1897 and 1899) and was placed on the ballot for voters to consider at the 6 November 1900 election. As a result of the election, in which the amendment received 240,031 votes in favor and 144,072 tallies against, sterner standards were established.

On an appeal from a Hoosier who failed to meet the tougher requirements, however, the Indiana Supreme Court during its November 1900 term ruled in the case *In re Denny* that although the amendment received more yes than no votes, it had failed to pass because it did not receive a majority of *all* the votes cast in the general election. Furthermore, since the amendment had been neither approved nor defeated, but was still pending a decision by the voters, the 1851 Constitution stated that "no additional amendment or amendments could be proposed," which effectively blocked any other attempt at constitutional reform.[17]

Such an impasse proved to be intolerable to a reformer like Dunn, who also saw in the constitutional roadblock a unique opportunity to enhance the Democratic party's chances for success in future elections. In a speech before the Indiana Democratic Club in December 1908 Dunn pointed out that in a ten-year period from 1894 to 1904, other states had adopted two hundred and thirty constitutional amendments while Indiana had failed to pass successfully even one. Dunn blamed the framers of the 1851 Constitution for tying "the hands of posterity too tightly. They seemed to have the idea that wisdom would die with them." He regarded the process for attaining constitutional amendments as a safety valve that should be "so adjusted as not to be a mere escape pipe for passing fancy or political prejudice, but at the same time should not require so much force to move it as is liable to explode the boiler."[18]

To relieve what he regarded as a potentially explosive situation, the Hoosier historian lent his expertise to the Marshall administration by devising a novel, for Indiana and the rest of the nation, approach to constitutional reform. The first hints of what was to come appeared prior to a Democratic caucus the night of 13 February 1911. Although what was to be discussed at the meeting was theoretically supposed to be a secret, the *Indianapolis News* reported that one of the issues to be considered was the state's constitution. The newspaper noted unconfirmed reports that "an entirely new Constitution is to be proposed, another that certain phases of the document are to be gone over, and still another to the effect that the caucus will be asked to consider ways for making easier the method of amending the Constitution, if a way is found possible."[19]

The *News*'s sources were accurate; the next day Marshall announced that the caucus had approved the idea of submitting an act to the General Assembly providing for an entirely new constitution—a method that had not been used successfully in the United States since the eighteenth century.[20] Marshall rationalized such an action on the grounds that the Declaration of Independence granted the people the right to change the method and form of their government. The changes included in the new constitution, the governor asserted, had been decided upon after consultations with a group of Indiana attorneys. One of those lawyers, whom Marshall failed to identify by name, advised him that if he studied the existing Indiana constitution he could find a means "to accomplish what I felt should be accomplished, and thus to get around the vexing question of whether there is a proposed amendment before the people."[21]

The attorney Marshall refused to name was Dunn, who outlined his role in the matter in his history of the state, *Indiana and Indianans*. Dunn, who had praised Marshall's previous course of noninterference in other departments of government, reversed himself on this issue. He argued that the "radical action" of submitting a new constitution to be acted on by the General Assembly was called for in order to cut the Gordian knot blocking constitutional reform. "The plan struck me as feasible, and he [Marshall] asked me to formulate the changes which I considered desirable, which I did," Dunn recalled.[22]

Direct action in the legislative process was, of course, nothing new to this political historian who had served a similar role in the Australian ballot and Indianapolis city charter issues. In fact, to Dunn's way of thinking a historian had an obligation to act when he saw a problem in government. "If you want intelligent legislation," he reasoned, "you must first find out just what is wrong, and then devise the remedy for that wrong."[23]

In drafting his constitutional proposal, Dunn depended upon his historical knowledge and the skills he learned as an attorney and not on any detailed correspondence from Marshall. Caroline Dunn has suggested that since both her father and the governor lived in Indianapolis and were long-time Democrats, it would have been more likely for them to discuss an issue like reforming the constitution in person, rather than through the mail or by memo.[24] She also noted that during Marshall's term as governor, her family and the Marshalls lived just a few blocks away from one another on Pennsylvania Street (Dunn's home was at 915 North Pennsylvania, while the Marshalls lived at 1219 North Pennsylvania).[25]

The legal right to produce a new constitution for the legislature to consider, claimed Dunn, rested upon the original document's statements that "the people have, at all times, an indefeasible right to alter and reform their government," and that the "legislative authority of the state shall be vested in the General Assembly."[26] Dunn pointed out that Indiana's 1816 Constitution contained no process for amending the document. The only rationale for replacing it, besides the people's inherent right to do so, was a provision it contained whereby every twelve years after the constitution had taken effect a vote would be taken to see if people were for or against calling a constitutional convention.[27]

Neither the first twelve-year vote in 1828, nor the second in 1840, produced a majority of voters in favor of calling a constitutional convention. It took the collapse of Indiana's internal improvements scheme in the late 1840s to lead Hoosiers to seek a new constitution through a constitutional convention in 1850–51.[28] When considering the amendment process for the new constitution, however, convention delegates realized the session had failed to meet the procedures outlined for such matters in the 1816 Constitution. With that in mind, Dunn argued that the delegates' aim was not to "limit the right of revision, but to extend it by the system of special amendment." He went on to claim:

It is evident that the provisions for amendment . . . are not intended as any limitation on the right of the people to adopt a new constitution whenever they so desire. . . . The only restriction is that if they desire to proceed by special amendment . . . they must follow strictly the method there provided, in order to make the amendment valid.[29]

To those who charged that the "new" constitution was no more than a series of amendments to the existing constitution and, therefore, had to be dealt with by the amending procedures outlined in the 1851 document, Dunn said that they were confused about the "ordinary and the legal meaning of terms." He gave as an example the changing of a will. If someone had made and then rewritten a will, "it would be a new will; but if the change were added as a codicil it would be an amended will." The proposed constitution he drew up in 1911, Dunn argued, had to be considered as a new one "from the standpoint of the diversity of its effects."[30]

The document Dunn produced and Marshall presented to the General Assembly for debate included such earlier reform attempts as granting the legislature the power to fix requirements for admission to the bar and increasing the size of the Indiana Supreme Court from five justices to as many as eleven. Other revisions included increasing the size of the Indiana House of Representatives to one hundred and thirty members; lengthening the General Assembly session to one hundred days; giving the legislature the power to enact workmen's compensation laws and measures for the initiative, referendum, and recall of all elected officials, except judges; requiring a three-fifths vote by the House and Senate to override a governor's veto; giving the governor line-item veto power on appropriation bills; prohibiting salary increases for public officials during the term to which they were elected; easing the amending process for the Indiana constitution; and providing political parties the opportunity to declare for or against constitutional amendments at their conventions and making such a decision a part of their tickets to be acted on by voters.[31]

Although Dunn's constitution provided for the initiative, referendum, and recall of public officials—mainstays of Progressive Era political reform efforts—Marshall, enhancing his image as a cautious reformer, approved the placement of that clause in the new constitution with "no intention upon my part that it should ever be used." He offered as an example someone approaching a set of railroad tracks. Even if the tracks were not equipped with warning signals, a person in "sound mind" would know some danger existed in crossing the tracks. According to the governor, the initiative, referendum, and recall clause was put in Dunn's document "not for use but to sharply call the attention of the Legislator to the fact that he was the representative of the people and not the representative of a special interest and that he would better walk carefully or such a condition of affairs might arise as to make it necessary for the people to pass upon their own laws."[32]

For Dunn, however, the chief purpose of the new constitution was "to secure honest elections," without which, he argued, government would be "a sham and a mockery."[33] As with the Australian ballot measure, his underlying reason for attempting to create an honest electorate was simple: it would translate into election success for the Democratic party. Dunn earnestly believed that given a choice between the Democrat and Republican programs, an honest, intelligent voter could not help but vote for the Democrats. What better way to ensure Democratic party success at the polls than to provide an environment in which the Democratic voter could prosper? He even went so far as to charge that Republican opposition to the new constitution, which offered a "speedy and inexpensive" way to secure an honest electorate, was based on the GOP's "knowledge that it [the new constitution] will injure that party politically."[34]

Like many Progressive Era reform proposals, however, Dunn's document was tainted by nativism, especially in its voting eligibility requirements.[35] The new constitution restricted voting rights to male citizens of the United States above twenty-one years of age who had resided in the state for twelve months, in a township for sixty days, and in a precinct for thirty days preceding an election. (Under the then existing constitution, every male of foreign birth above twenty-one years of age who had declared his intention to become a United States citizen and had resided in the state for six months, and in the country for one year, was eligible to vote.) Dunn's measure also limited suffrage by insisting that voters pay their poll tax the year of any election, and, after 1 November 1913, it stipulated that Hoosiers who could "not read in English or some other known tongue any section of the Constitution of the State" would not be allowed to register to vote.[36]

Limiting suffrage to educated citizens became a common proposal during the Progressive Era. A. James Reichley claims that a number of Progressives shared the Founding Fathers' belief that "republican government would be unworkable without well-informed, independent voters who cast their ballots for what is best for the nation as a whole" —a citizenship description many immigrants failed to fit.[37] Also, the proposed Indiana constitution's limit on voting rights to those who could read or write paralleled a national movement's attempt to require a literacy test for immigrants. First introduced in Congress in 1895, the literacy measure made its way through the House and Senate in 1897, 1913, 1915, and 1917. Vetoed by Presidents Grover Cleveland, William Howard Taft, and Woodrow Wilson, the test was enacted by Congress over Wilson's veto in 1917. The new law, however, as John Higham has pointed out, "proved a fairly coarse sieve," since rising literacy rates in Europe blunted the law's impact.[38]

Dunn presented a point-by-point defense of the restrictive voting eligibility requirements contained in his document during a speech before the American Political Science Association's 1911 annual meeting. An education test for suffrage was essential, he argued, because if illiterates were permitted to vote, someone would have to mark the ballot for them, which eliminated the secret ballot and could make vote buying easier. Also, a poll tax was needed because, according to Dunn, a "large part of the class who sell their votes are included in the class who do not pay their poll taxes."[39]

As to the tightening of residential standards, Dunn pointed out that the 1851 Constitution gave immigrants with six-months residence in the state, and who had declared their intention to become United States citizens, the right to vote because the state wanted to encourage immigrants to settle within its borders.[40] In recent years, however, Dunn claimed that there appeared in Indiana "a large class of immigrants who have no real intent to become citizens, but only to accumulate enough money for comfortable living in their native countries." Since these immigrants were interested only in making money, Dunn said, they were often more than happy to sell their franchise for cash. "In fact," he added, "they are commonly 'Naturalized' in blocks, by political parties that have already bargained for their votes."[41]

The dishonest elections resulting from such rampant bribery and vote selling were "sapping the very life of this nation today," Dunn told the association members. Such Progressive attempts to remedy the ills of government as the initiative, referendum, and recall; commission government; and the short ballot were "only salves applied to the skin to cure a blood disease." He believed that the only way to obtain good government was to ensure honest elections. Dunn asked those assembled:

> What do direct primaries amount to, if the voters are bought? What are the initiative, referendum, or recall if the appeal is to a debauched electorate? What is commission government, if the commissioners can buy their elections? What difference whether a man vote a long or short ballot, if his vote is sold? Of what avail to try to control the "big business" of the country, so long as we allow it, by the supply of campaign funds, to buy the election of men who will serve it? The first and greatest requisite—the one without which all others amount to nothing—is the purification of elections.[42]

Marshall echoed Dunn's fears about "aliens" somehow besmirching the sanctity of the ballot box. Discussing the new constitution with a fellow Democrat, Marshall said that after consulting others, he believed that it was "advisable to see if we could not try to limit the suffrage in Indiana by a new Constitution."[43] During a June 1911 speech before the Indiana Democratic Editorial Association in La Porte, Marshall reminded his audience that voting "was not an inalienable right." The governor termed unrestricted suffrage as "one of the [most] dangerous experiments in government." The governor stated that a great number of foreigners had come into the state and, aided by unnamed "political manipulators," had polluted the purity of the ballot box and threatened to menace American civilization.[44]

Perhaps secretly agreeing with Dunn's assessment that "honest" elections could mean trouble for the GOP at the polls, the Republican response to the new constitution was overwhelmingly hostile. GOP leaders in the Indiana House and Senate blasted the measure calling it a "one-man constitution" and claiming that Marshall was usurping the people's rights. Sen. William Wood of Lafayette derided the fact that the legislation was agreed upon at a party caucus and not by the people, and he also argued that "there is not a single member of this Legislature that was selected for the purpose of framing a constitution." Rep. Jesse Eschbach of Warsaw, House minority leader, called the governor's action "contemptible" and claimed it marked "the last gasp of what promised to be a period of Democratic power and prestige, a puerile attempt to bolster up fallen political power and to conceal the failure and blundering of two years of Democratic supremacy."[45]

Sen. James Sexson of Owen County went one step farther than his GOP colleagues. On 16 February 1911 Sexson introduced a Senate resolution appointing Marshall as a committee of one with the power to put the new constitution into effect without holding an election. The resolution also gave the Democratic governor the power to "revise the Lord's prayer, amend the Declaration of Independence, repeal the Mosaic Law, bring the Thirty-Nine Articles of Faith down to date, abridge the Sermon on the Mount, and do all other things as will appear in his infinite wisdom and supreme interest in the welfare of the people, to be fitting and proper." The *Indianapolis Star* reported to its readers that Democratic senators said nothing after the resolution had been called out of order, but "the Republicans were still smiling broadly when they adjourned." Although his proposal failed to pass muster, Sexson did get something for his efforts—pats on the back from amused GOP legislators.[46]

The GOP's assault on the new constitution received daily coverage in the *Indianapolis Star*, which supported the Republican party editorially. The newspaper constantly hammered away at the proposed plan and its architects, giving front-page coverage to attacks on Marshall from former GOP governors Winfield T. Durbin and J. Frank Hanly and providing the same prominent space to a group of lawyers who viewed the measure as unconstitutional.[47] The *Star*, however, saved its biggest broadsides against the plan for its editorial pages. Recalling Marshall's campaign speeches in which the candidate claimed to be a strict constructionist when it came to executive authority, the newspaper asked why in this instance Marshall turned his back on his stated beliefs. Although the *Star* suggested the possibility that the governor planned to use the issue of a new constitution as a way to promote a run for the White House in 1912, it nevertheless concluded that Marshall was "a man urged on by imperious circumstances to do that against which his whole nature revolts. It must be hard for a sensitive man to do something that he feels instinctively is wrong."[48]

The *Star* hinted in its editorial pages that Dunn was the person to blame for pushing Marshall down the path of constitutional ruin. Calling Dunn "advisor to the throne and oracular interpreter of all constitutions," the editorial also damned him for his "unerring inaccuracy" on constitutional matters. The newspaper went on to state that Democrats like Dunn and Marshall worshipped a "tin god" called "powers not delegated." Anyone using such powers, the editorial added, was "fit for nothing less terrible than boiling oil."[49]

In spite of these partisan attacks and complaints from some special interest groups (women suffragists and prohibitionists) that their agendas were being ignored, Dunn stood firmly behind his proposal. He produced a number of articles defending the new constitution for the Democratic-leaning *Indianapolis News*, which, along with the *Indianapolis Sun* (a politically independent newspaper), supported the constitutional reform effort. Dunn's *News* articles outlining the case for the new constitution were eventually combined into a pamphlet titled *The Proposed Constitution of Indiana*. In the articles he acknowledged the protests of those interest groups left out of the legislation, but he pointed out that their concerns could be addressed in the future because the amendment process would be much easier under the new constitution. He also said that those people who liked the changes but opposed the way in which the new constitution was submitted had a simple method for registering their complaint—the ballot box. "If you really believe that 'it is a good meal, but it came through the wrong hopper,'" advised Dunn, "the sensible course is to take the meal and save your condemnation for the hopper."[50]

Along with Dunn, Marshall kept busy defending the effort to change the state's highest law. The Republican onslaught against the measure hardened the governor's support for

Dunn's work. "A theory must fall in the face of a condition," Marshall responded to those who said he was turning his back on his stated belief that each branch of government keep to its own business. Once someone discovers a theory he held was incorrect, the governor added, he should not "be condemned for forsaking a theory to meet a practical problem of government as it now is."[51] In a letter to Democratic congressman Henry Barnhart, Marshall noted the outcry over the issue but reasoned that "the way the Republicans are jumping on it [the new constitution] convinces me that it must have some merit in it."[52] In a later letter to the congressman, the governor outlined his other, more economically based, reasons for backing Dunn's work:

> While the lawyers amendment is pending, we can propose no additional amendments. To get rid of it would perhaps cost $100,000.00 in a special election. To call a constitutional convention might cost half a million dollars and nothing be accomplished. The proposed changes are so slight as to not shock anybody when they are considered, can be passed upon by the people without a single cent of expense; if rejected, no harm is done, if approved, an easy way is opened up for all future changes in the constitution which the people may desire. If the method is illegal and improper, of course, the courts are open to stop the same. I am quite sure that all good citizens desire a more stringent regulation of the franchise.[53]

Along with the cost, Marshall feared that due to the widely divergent views in Indiana on such reform issues as prohibition, equal suffrage, and the initiative, referendum, and recall, any constitutional convention "would be fraught with great danger and would shake the state into a great passion." He also foresaw that a convention would be filled with partisan bickering, a prediction the governor said was substantiated by the GOP assaults on the new constitution.[54]

James A. Woodburn, an Indiana University professor of history and department chairman, disagreed with Marshall's view that a constitutional convention might become too partisan. Instead, Woodburn described the new constitution as "too unusual and too partisan." He predicted that if the document made its way to the voters for their decision at the polls, it would be defeated by as many as one hundred thousand votes. "Three parties," he wrote Grace Julian Clarke, active in the state's women's suffrage movement, "will oppose it in conventions,—Republicans, Socialists and Prohibitionists."[55] Later, during a 5 May 1913 speech to the Woman's Franchise League of Indiana, Woodburn conceded that the Indiana constitution's amendment process was "absurd," but recommended a different approach than Dunn's for improving the document. The Indiana University professor advocated letting "the people decide in the good old way—through men elected for the purpose, their accredited representative in convention assembled—what changes shall be proposed in their constitutional organic law." Although he acknowledged that such a convention might produce some disagreements, Woodburn noted that "out of it all will come the common judgment, and by that we can afford to abide."[56]

Dunn, who often acted as the governor's mouthpiece in the matter of the new constitution, gave other reasons for Marshall's support. As a lawyer himself, the governor, Dunn argued, had expressed concern that the existing five-member Indiana Supreme Court was too small to handle what had become a large caseload. Other issues Marshall supported that were blocked by what Dunn termed "an antiquated constitution" included the passage of a workmen's compensation law and an easier method for the state to condemn property.[57]

As the Dunn constitution made its way through the General Assembly, the courts seemed to be the only roadblock left. Introduced by Sen. Evan Stotsenburg, Senate Bill No. 407—despite Republican efforts in the Senate's Committee on Constitutional Revision to indefinitely postpone action on the matter—passed the Senate on 27 February 1911. A similar situation occurred in the House, where the bill survived further GOP attempts at postponement. Partisan feelings ran so high that during the third reading of the bill in the House Republican representative Elmer Oldaker of Wayne County announced that some of the Democrats "ought to be hanged." Incensed by Oldaker's statement, Democratic representative Harry Strickland of Hancock

Marion County Circuit Court judge Charles Remster

County challenged his colleague to a fight in the House cloakroom. Fortunately, cooler heads prevailed, and the two men were separated before any punches were thrown.[58] On 2 March 1911 the House approved the new constitution. Two days later Marshall signed the bill into law.

Opponents of the constitution, frustrated at being unable to stop it at the legislative level, turned to the judicial branch for relief. John Dye and Addison Harris, two Republican attorneys who Dunn claimed had attempted to block previous Democratic reform legislation, sought a Marion County Circuit Court injunction preventing the State Election Board from placing the new Indiana constitution question on the ballot in the 1912 election.[59] Judge Charles Remster, a Democrat, granted the injunction, and the case ended up in the Indiana Supreme Court.

This temporary judicial setback sparked Dunn to lobby vigorously on behalf of his measure. Restating his firm belief in the need for honest elections, Dunn said the movement to reform Indiana's constitution was fated to succeed despite Judge Remster's decision and the upholding of that decision by the state's highest court—an action he anticipated because the supreme court had a Republican majority. Because the attempt at constitutional revision was what he called a "moral reform movement" (a familiar argument made by reformers during the Progressive Era), neither court decisions nor any other obstacles could halt its eventual success "any more than the anti-slavery movement was stopped by the Dred Scott decision."[60]

On 5 July 1912 Dunn's prediction of the high court's decision came to pass, but with a twist. By a slim one-vote majority the Indiana Supreme Court upheld Judge Remster's decision. The court's decision crossed party lines, as two Republican judges were joined by a Democrat in the majority opinion. That Democrat, Chief Justice Charles Cox, in writing the majority opinion, said the case's main question was whether or not creating a new constitution was "a valid exercise of legislative power by the General Assembly."[61]

Cox ruled that the "legislative authority" granted to the General Assembly by the constitution did not include the power to replace or amend the document unless the legislature followed the process already outlined in the 1851 Indiana Constitution. Although acknowledging the potential need for revising the document, Cox maintained that if the people of the state believed some changes were needed, they could make them by following the procedure already spelled out in the existing constitution. "That they had not done so, and that the General Assembly may believe good will follow by deviating from the slow and orderly processes, will not justify a construction of the Constitution which does violence to its intent and express provisions," wrote Cox.[62]

Dissenting from the majority's viewpoint, Justice Douglas Morris believed that the court had overstepped its authority by killing the new constitution before it could be voted on by Hoosiers. The court, he wrote, had the power to decide whether or not a statute had been legally adopted, but it could not "restrain the enactment of an unconstitutional law." To issue an injunction in this case, he added, would prohibit the legislature and electors from exercising their *"legislative duty."* He used as an example a messenger from the General Assembly taking a bill that had already been passed by that body to the governor. "Would anyone imagine," Morris asked, "[that] the progress of the messenger could be arrested by an injunction? The inquiry answers itself." He saw no distinction between the situation he outlined and the court's action in stopping a vote on the new constitution.[63]

This dissenting view was echoed by Marshall, who took a page from his opponents on the issue by calling the court's action "a clear usurpation of authority." In his autobiography, the governor said that he had never intended that, if the new constitution were ratified by Hoosier voters, the question of the measure's constitutionality could not be raised by anyone who felt himself injured by its passage. He called the court's majority opinion the most "flagrant interference on the part of the judicial with the rights, privileges and duties of the legislative and executive branches of government."[64]

Urged by many friends and advisers to ignore the court's decision and place the constitution question on the ballot, Marshall instead decided to obey the majority's opinion. In reflecting on the controversy he said:

> I did not feel that I could afford to show any disrespect to the majority of the Supreme Court of the State of Indiana, or to lessen the respect in which I was teaching the people to hold the court's opinions, by myself openly flaunting one of its opinions.[65]

Instead of openly defying the court's decision, Marshall turned to the United States Supreme Court for relief. His appeal alleged that the Indiana Supreme Court's ruling on the new constitution denied the people of the nineteenth state a "republican form of government." Before the United States Supreme Court could hear his case, however, Marshall left the governor's office for another elected position—that of vice president under Woodrow Wilson. Due to what Marshall termed a "technicality" (the appeal failed to substitute his successor's name for his own), his appeal was de-

(Left to right) Indiana governor Thomas R. Marshall; Col. John P. Caldwell of Titusville, Pennsylvania; New Jersey governor Woodrow Wilson; Hugh Dougherty of Indianapolis; and W. C. Miller of Indianapolis at the 1912 Democratic National Convention in Baltimore, where Wilson received the nomination as president and Marshall was selected for the vice presidential slot

nied on 1 December 1913. Later, meeting one of the justices of the Supreme Court at a Washington dinner party, Marshall asked him why the Court had dismissed the case. The vice president quoted the justice as admitting that Marshall was right and the Indiana Supreme Court wrong on the constitution issue. But the justice went on to say that it was the policy of the Court "not to interfere, if it can avoid doing so, in any political questions arising in any of the states of the Union."[66] That action greatly pleased a leading opponent of the new constitution, the *Indianapolis Star*, which praised the Court's action and hoped that the ruling would discourage "dark lantern methods in the revision of constitutions."[67]

Blocked by the judicial branch of government in his plan for a new constitution, Dunn, like Marshall, vented his wrath at the Indiana Supreme Court's decision. Ever the reformer, and someone who hated to lose on any issue, he lamented the lack of any checks or balances on judicial power. Dunn said that until the American people rid themselves "of the absurd delusion that all judges are upright, and incorruptible, and infallible, and above partisan control, they will simply continue to suffer any indignities that the courts may choose to inflict upon them."[68]

The defeat of Dunn's new constitution, to which Marshall had so closely allied himself, actually helped the governor's subsequent political career. The furor over the Marshall administration's campaign for constitutional reform was "very instrumental," in Dunn's mind, in securing for Marshall the vice presidential nomination at the Democratic party's national convention in Baltimore. The often rancorous debate on the issue succeeded in advertising Marshall's name "from one end of the nation to the other." Dunn further theorized that the governor's support for such a progressive measure helped to alter perennial Democratic presidential candidate William Jennings Bryan's view of Marshall as a "reactionary."[69]

Dunn eventually left Indiana for service in Washington as private secretary to United States senator Samuel M. Ralston. Reform of the state's constitution, however, continued to attract the historian's interest. In 1921, at a meeting of the Indiana Democratic Club of Indianapolis, Dunn blasted three of thirteen amendments offered to the constitution by the Republican party (especially an amendment allowing blacks to serve in the state militia) and mourned the defeat of his earlier legislation. If the 1911 Constitution had not been halted by what Dunn called "unwarrantable court interference," the state could ignore the ten "unobjectionable amendments" and could have been "spared the humiliation during the late war of having alien enemies entitled to vote under its constitution. We are in position to say: 'I told you so;' and Democrats ought to feel free to say it."[70]

The Republican amendment allowing African Americans to serve in the Indiana militia brought out the worst in Dunn. If a black militia company was sent to quell a labor dispute, Dunn warned, a race riot would break out and the "streets of Indianapolis will run blood on account of it." He also noted that although Indianapolis contained "a large population of orderly and well-disposed negro citizens," the city for years had also been a "haven for the criminal classes expelled from other places, and especially from the South."[71]

The Indiana historian's racial bias (when it came to voting rights) had been displayed years earlier in another Indiana Democratic Club speech. During that talk Dunn ridiculed a GOP party platform plank calling for a reduction in both congressional and electoral college representation for states that unconstitutionally limited voting rights. "Suffrage," Dunn claimed, has "debased the negro, on the average, instead of elevating him. It has given him false ideas of citizenship. It has made him insolent and quarrelsome instead of self-respecting." Because he believed that the right to vote was based on the state's welfare, it would be unkind to give blacks "a right that is injuring him and injuring the State also." It was no injustice, he continued, to deny suffrage "to the negro who remains illiterate, shiftless or criminal."[72] Of course, this screed against African-American suffrage might have been prompted by the propensity of blacks to vote, when they could, for the party of Lincoln—the GOP—as opposed to Dunn's Democratic party, which had fought desperately in Indiana following the Civil War to deny blacks the right to vote.[73]

Notwithstanding Dunn's fulminations against the Republican-backed constitutional amendments, one of them was similar to an amendment he had backed ten years earlier. Amendment One, which was the only one of the thirteen amendments to pass in the 1921 special election (130,242 for the measure versus 80,574 against), limited suffrage in Indiana to United States citizens, either native born or fully naturalized. On 1 March 1921 Gov. Warren T. McCray declared the amendment adopted.[74] The suffrage amendment survived a court challenge questioning whether it had been approved by "a majority of electors of the state." The Indiana Supreme Court ruled in the case of *Simmons v. Bird, et al.* that a majority of electors meant a "majority of the electors who vote at the election at which an amendment is submitted for ratification." The amendment, the court said, had been "properly adopted, regardless of the fact that there may have been a much greater number of qualified electors in the state than the number of those who actually voted at the special election."[75]

It took another fourteen years, however, for the Indiana Supreme Court to ease further its strict interpretation of whether an amendment to the state constitution had been passed by the voters. In the case *In re Todd*, the court ruled that a proposed amendment became a part of the constitution if it received "a majority of those votes cast for and against its adoption"—a much easier standard to meet than the one established by the *In re Denny* decision.[76]

The Indiana constitution as it existed in 1911 was outdated, and Dunn's document contained measures that are considered commonplace today. Still, constitutional scholars have recommended against allowing legislatures to make wholesale changes to a state's constitution; they have preferred the more standard approach of having lawmakers offer a few amendments or call for a special constitutional convention to make the needed revisions.[77] Constitutional theorists have argued that a legislative body has neither the time nor expertise necessary to craft a new constitution for a state. Also, they cite the possibility that lawmakers' actions might be "colored by political considerations." The political party in power could "exert undue political influence in rewriting the fundamental law." A constitutional convention would be influenced less likely by outside pressures in its deliberations and more likely to be independent in its judgment than legislators who are "active participants in the political arena."[78]

Dunn's admitted attempts to limit suffrage through the new constitution in order to gain a partisan advantage come election time were antidemocratic, especially his attempt to limit alleged foreign and minority influence at the polls through a poll tax and literacy requirements. The Indiana Supreme Court did, however, overstep its authority when it ruled Dunn's document unconstitutional even before it could be considered by Hoosier voters.

Whatever the problems with his means, Dunn, not Marshall, should receive credit for conjuring up a unique method for attempting to change what has been called a "'stage coach' era Constitution." Before more liberal methods for constitutional changes were adopted, revisions in the state's highest law had proceeded at a glacial pace. From the 1850s to the 1930s the Indiana General Assembly considered approximately four hundred changes to the constitution. Of that number, twenty-five were considered by voters at the polls and only nine were approved, seven of which passed at an 1881 special election.[79]

The national movement to tighten suffrage requirements, which Dunn championed in Indiana with his new constitution, did have an effect on voting patterns. The introduction of the Australian ballot system and tighter registration and literacy requirements, combined with the weakening hold of political parties on voters, worked together to lower voter turnout from 79 percent of eligible voters in the 1896 presidential election to 49 percent in 1924. Even in Indiana, where party competition remained fairly even until the 1920s, voter turnout declined from 95 percent of those eligible in 1896 to 78 percent by the 1912 election.[80] Whether these lower turnouts consisted of the intelligent electorate Dunn desired is difficult to discern, but if they did he would have been disappointed with the results. From 1917 to 1933, Hoosier voters elected Republicans as governor.

6

Dunn and the Preservation of the Miami Indian Language

THE FRUSTRATIONS DUNN MUST HAVE FELT OVER THE FAILURE
of adoption of his new Indiana constitution may have been
lessened by his continuing work on a subject that intrigued
him throughout the early twentieth century—the language of the Miami Indians of Indiana. Even while working on such massive projects as his two-volume study of Indianapolis, Dunn found time to collect information on the
history of Native Americans in Indiana, which appeared as
a series of newspaper articles in the *Indianapolis News*
and later, in 1908, as the book *True Indian Stories*. The
book featured investigations of the lives of such well-
known Native Americans as Little Turtle and Tecumseh,
as well as a glossary of Indiana Indian names researched
by Dunn.

Throughout his life Dunn attempted to convince historical societies and other organizations around the country to
preserve the language of the Potawatomi, Shawnee, and Miami nations. When considering the enormous effort that
had been made to rescue the languages of Egypt, Babylon,
and other ancient lands, Dunn said that "it should arouse a
realization of the importance of preserving the living languages of our own country while there is yet time, and especially so because these are not written languages, and if
once lost they are lost forever." These languages were worth
preserving, said the historian, not only because of the influence they have had on "our own language, but also for their
intrinsic merit."[1]

Little Turtle

As he had with other reform efforts, Dunn attempted to enlighten the public on an issue that, in this case the preservation of Indian languages, it knew practically nothing about. This lack of awareness on the public's part did not surprise Dunn, who viewed such a situation as natural considering that the public's prevalent ideas about Native Americans were derived chiefly from novels such as James Fenimore Cooper's *The Last of the Mohicans* (1826) and poems such as Henry Wadsworth Longfellow's *The Song of Hiawatha*. These works were "more responsible for American opinions of the Indians and their customs and beliefs than all of the scientific works on the subject that have ever been published."[2] Dunn set out to change that.

During Dunn's lifetime, the majority of the Miami, an estimated five hundred people, still lived in northern Indiana. A lesser number, about seventy-five in 1900, resided in the Indian territory (now Oklahoma). By the beginning of the twentieth century few Miami in Indiana spoke the language of their ancestors. English, noted Stewart Rafert in his history of Indiana's Miami Indians, became "the language to be learned if one wanted to advance to higher status or to integrate more thoroughly into the dominant society."[3] Along with a dwindling population of native speakers, another difficulty was the "extraordinary ignorance" displayed by Americans in regard to this field, said Dunn. The obvious reason for this sorry situation, he claimed, was that there existed "no practical or pecuniary profit in it."[4]

All of these potential roadblocks, however, failed to deter Dunn from his Native American language studies. According to Caroline Dunn, one of her father's sisters once remarked to her that Dunn had always been interested in Indians, "much more so than most people." Also, because her father possessed an "intellectual curiosity to a great degree," Caroline noted that studying a nearly extinct Indian language would appeal to her father's "inquiring and reasoning type of mind."[5]

Along with his earlier work on the conflicts between settlers and Native Americans in the West, in which he had to translate numerous Indian names and terms, Dunn had delved a bit into Native American lore and language in his second book, *Indiana: A Redemption from Slavery*, published in 1888. In that work Dunn described the different dialects of the Algonquin tribes along the Wabash River, and he also revealed some of his research methods. Discussing the derivation of the word Wabash, he notes that Webster's dictionary of his time mistakenly defined Wabash as "a cloud blown forward by an equinoctial wind." Unable to track down the source for the error, Dunn nevertheless theorized that it came from "mistaking an illustration for a definition." As an example he pointed to a letter he had once received from an Indian agent from whom he had sought the meaning of a word. The agent had responded that the word "signified a 'mushroom or toadstool.' On further inquiry he said that it meant 'anything white,' and that the Indian to whom he had first spoken had answered by pointing to a toadstool," Dunn said.[6]

The interest and expertise Dunn displayed in Indian languages caught the eye of fellow Hoosier James Mooney, who worked for the Smithsonian Institution's Bureau of American Ethnology in Washington, D.C. In a letter to Dunn, Mooney wrote that he had read a copy of *Indiana: A Redemption from Slavery*. Mooney said the work gave him a great deal of pleasure, particularly because its author took such pains to "secure correctness in the Indian portions." The ethnologist went on to write that the death of a "few thousand savages" was of very little significance in the development of a state, but their history was important as one part of the state's history because Indian mythology and religious practices "give us the starting point in the development of human thought & their local & personal names—correctly stated—afford valuable material to the linguist."[7] By the time Dunn's collection of articles on Native Americans, *True Indian Stories*, was published, the Indiana historian had garnered for himself the distinction of being, according to a reviewer in the *American Anthropologist*, the country's "most competent authority on all that relates to the Indian tribes of the Ohio Valley."[8]

Francis Godfroy

Pursuing his glossary of Indiana Indian names for his *True Indian Stories*, Dunn fell in love with the speech patterns of Native Americans and hit on a point he would make again and again: namely, the language's intrinsic value as a language. "The grammatical inflections of Algonquian words are more refined and present nicer distinctions of meaning," said Dunn, "not only than those of the English, but also than those of any European language." If anyone dared to doubt his statement, he referred him to the conjugation of the verb "waub" of the Ojibwa, which covered ninety quarto pages. And yet, Dunn continued, as complicated as the language might seem, it was based on a "very simple and rational linguistic system," which expressed through verbal inflection the same exact ideas that "we express through various forms of circumlocution."[9]

Of course, Dunn had the aid of a number of Native Americans in conducting his language work. He worked most closely with Gabriel Godfroy, who, according to Dunn, was "the best Miami interpreter in Indiana." Born near

Hartford City, Indiana, on 1 January 1834, Godfroy was
the son of Francis Godfroy, a French Miami half blood, and
Sakakwatah, a Miami woman. Francis Godfroy operated a
trading post until his death in 1840. The Godfroy family
was allowed to remain in Indiana, near Peru, when about
half the tribe was taken west during the Miami removal in
1846. As a youngster Gabriel had been sent by his father
to Vincennes for instruction by M. Bellier, whom Dunn
called "the village pedagogue." Within a week, however,
the young Miami was so homesick that he was sent home.
Once safely home, Godfroy grew to become "an amiable,
honorable gentleman, who bore adversity bravely, and was
universally respected," noted Dunn. Godfroy was esteemed
by both his fellow Miami and whites in the area, with his
home serving as a de facto community center for both
groups. Later, Godfroy's generous nature led to severe financial difficulties as he became embroiled on behalf of fellow Miami in costly litigation with the county government
involving taxation of Miami treaty lands.[10]

As an older man, Godfroy was described by George S.
Cottman as "picturesque in appearance and literatesque in
character." Cottman, an amateur historian in his own right
and a frequent chronicler of Hoosier history for various Indianapolis newspapers, wrote in a story on the Miami living
near Peru in 1900 that Godfroy, then in his sixties, was a
powerfully built man with "a massive, strong face made leo-
nine by a heavy growth of yellowish-white hair which falls
to the shoulders or is worn in a knot behind." Although
Cottman reported that Godfroy told him tales about the
wrongs done to his tribe by whites in the past, Dunn managed to win Godfroy's trust, working closely with him during the last five years of the Miami's life (Godfroy died on 14
August 1910).[11]

In these meetings, Dunn learned more about the tribe's
language and customs. Godfroy may have had no formal
schooling, but Dunn noted that he did possess "a bright
mind and a fine memory," both of which aided him in his
work with the Indiana historian. "The book of nature was
very attractive to him," Dunn said, "and he became an en-

cyclopedia of forest lore and local history." Godfroy's excellence as an interpreter was also due, according to Dunn, to his general knowledge and "the fact that he knew English so well that he could think in it as well as in Miami. No Indian interpreter is very reliable until he reaches that point."[12]

In addition to his face-to-face encounters with Miami, Dunn also had help from other sources, most notably a German scholar who had been studying the tribe's language for many years. Dr. Albert Samuel Gatschet, who came to America in 1868 from his native Germany, had collected

Gabriel Godfroy, circa 1900

through the years a large body of information on Indian texts and vocabularies. A charter member of the Bureau of American Ethnology upon its organization in 1879, Gatschet shared much of his work with the bureau. Upon Gatschet's death in 1907, the bureau shared this material with Dunn, much of it on the Peoria language spoken by Algonquin Indians living in Illinois, in order for him to prepare a study on the Algonquian languages of the Middle West. In examining Gatschet's research, Dunn came to the conclusion that much of the Peoria language was really the common Western Miami language. He wrote William Henry Holmes at the bureau that Godfroy told him that Elizabeth Vallier, from whom Gatschet obtained a large portion of his material, was in fact "a Miami who was brought up near him; and that she did not leave Indiana until after she was a married woman."[13]

To confirm his theory Dunn made several trips to visit the Miami living in Oklahoma. Following his first trip west in the spring of 1909, he made subsequent visits in 1910, 1912, 1913, and 1914. As he had with Godfroy in Indiana, Dunn found a Miami in Oklahoma who proved to be invaluable in his work: Mrs. Sarah Wadsworth. Born near Kokomo, Indiana, and raised in the state, Wadsworth journeyed to Kansas with other Miami in 1873 and to Oklahoma two years later. "She is bright," Dunn said of her, "and fairly educated —reads English very well and showed intelligence in the grammatical inquiries I made of her." Luckily for Dunn, Wadsworth employed an old Miami housekeeper who did not speak English and "consequently her Miami is pretty fresh." In the summer of 1909 Wadsworth, while visiting relatives in Peru, stopped in Indianapolis to visit Dunn and worked with him on the Miami language for about a week. "I can dimly remember her when she was entertained in our home for dinner one evening during her stay here," Caroline Dunn said, "and an Indian bowl which she brought Mother as a gift was a cherished household possession for many years."[14]

Both Gatschet and Dunn also worked closely with another Oklahoma Indian, George Finley. Although a Piankashaw by descent, Finley proved to be of great help because

Godfroy family group portrait

he could speak the Peoria dialect, having lived among the Peoria people in Miami County, Kansas. Dunn also used the interpretive skills of Rev. Thomas Richardville, a great-grandson of the Miami chief Jean Baptiste Richardville.[15]

After his western trip in 1909, Dunn wrote Holmes at the Bureau of American Ethnology about his impressions from his time with the Miami and the future of the tribe's language. He said:

> I return deeply impressed with two things. The first is that the Miami is more nearly extinct than any of the great languages of the Middle West. Practically, it can hardly be called a spoken language today—I think it is talked less in Oklahoma than in Indiana, and everyone I have worked with complains of forgetting words on account of disuse. As mentioned, there is apparently nothing in print and whatever is done with the language must be done soon. The second is that the weak spot in the work done so far is the grammar, and especially of the verb, which, as you are aware is the chief feature of Indian grammar. Whatever is obtained in that line will simply have to be dug out; and I believe the wisest thing that could be done for the last of this year's work would be the study of the verb with Godfroy.[16]

(Left to right) Durand Godfroy with Gabriel Godfroy

Also in his letter to Holmes, Dunn, as he had done previously, lobbied hard for preserving the languages of all Native American tribes before it was too late. On the practical side, he noted that a better understanding of Indian languages would aid the work of philologists and archaeologists. Dunn said that these were "beautiful" ways to communicate, not composed, as many Americans seemed to think, of gestures and grunts, but "with inflections more extensive than the Greeks." In Dunn's opinion the Indian language was more "exact than any language I know of, and with peculiarities of construction differing from any other known languages. For a scientific knowledge of man their value cannot be overestimated."

From a more sentimental standpoint Dunn pointed out that many Indian languages were becoming extinct. Part of the reason for this was the Indian schools' concentration on their pupils learning English so that they could better make their way in the white world. Whites themselves, however, were just arriving at the point where they could "appreciate with some liberality of thought that these people fought our ancestors to hold the country that God had given them." Personally, Dunn believed it would be a disgrace to the entire nation to "let the languages of Pontiac, Tecumseh, Little Turtle, and the rest, perish from the face of the earth; but that is what is rapidly approaching."[17]

Dunn did all he could to keep Indian languages alive. In August 1910 Dunn, commissioned to do so by the Bureau of American Ethnology, journeyed to the John Carter Brown Library at Providence, Rhode Island, to examine a Peoria-French dictionary collected in Illinois by a French missionary priest in the eighteenth century. Aided by his Indian sources in Oklahoma, Dunn was able to fashion a Miami-English dictionary from the Peoria-French dictionary. Three sections were completed: "Abbaiser to Aimer," "Aller to Assomer," and "Assomer to Bercer." Sarah Wadsworth praised Dunn's work, noting upon seeing the manuscript: "This is real Indian; like I used to hear my mother and aunt talk when I was a child in Indiana."[18] Unfortunately, before it could be finished the bureau halted its support for the project.

Undeterred by this setback Dunn continued to work on compiling a Miami dictionary, which today is part of the Indiana State Library's collections and continues to be a valuable resource for a variety of researchers, from academics to present-day Miami. Between 1938 and 1940 Carl F. Voegelin, a linguist and later Indiana University distinguished professor of anthropology, edited Dunn's Miami manuscript dictionary and was able, thanks to funds provided by Indiana Historical Society board member and benefactor Eli Lilly, to publish the results in the Society's *Prehistory Research Series*. "I was immediately impressed with the late Mr. Dunn's orthography," Voegelin said, adding that he took very few editorial liberties with Dunn's work. He went on to note that the tendency of linguistic research in Dunn's time was to include for Indian languages symbols "representing details of sound out of all proportion to what the languages might require in making distinctions between words." Dunn, however, followed his "sound feeling on the matter, and boldly limited himself to a minimum of essential symbols."[19]

Years before Voegelin's efforts, Dunn had attempted to further his research on the subject by trying, in 1916, to create a Society for the Preservation of Indian Languages. To fund the organization, he hoped to raise, through letters and other personal appeals to individuals and institutions, approximately five to ten thousand dollars. Once such a society had been formed, according to Caroline Dunn, her father planned to "have this foundation publish the Peoria-French dictionary with English-Miami translation and various other manuscripts and texts which he had or he knew were obtainable."[20] The crying need in this field, Jacob Dunn believed, was not for essays and discussion but for "the presentation of the material in form available for the use of students."[21] Dunn was unable to raise the necessary funds, however, and his dream of a group working to preserve Indian languages never reached fruition.

As he had when his new Indiana constitution failed, Dunn felt no compunction about railing against those who he believed were responsible for frustrating his efforts to alleviate a wrong: in this instance, the failure to preserve Indian languages. He blasted the federal government's attempts in this area, calling them "curiously perverted." In his usual direct style, the amateur ethnologist also condemned the work of the ranking American ethnologists of his day claiming they were "groping in the dark" due to their reliance on the formulas of German philology, that, Dunn said, had "no more application to Indian languages than the rules of English grammar have to the Zulu or Chinese languages."[22]

Dunn always had been unafraid to speak his mind when it came to championing the Miami cause. As early as 1907 he even denigrated the work conducted by the government agency that later supported, for a time, his Miami language studies—the Bureau of American Ethnology. In an editorial for the *Indianapolis Star*, he blasted the agency's newest publication, *Handbook of American Indians*, particularly

A group of Miami pose at a Battle of Tippecanoe celebration

its sections on the Midwest. "There is [in the book] a compendious rehash of material that has been generally accessible for years and a few additions of error that can only be considered ludicrous," Dunn wrote. He pointed out that there were errors on such matters as the meaning of the name of a Potawatomi chief in Fulton County and the name of an Indian village near Fort Wayne. It was unfortunate, said Dunn, that the bureau did not take the time to consult the hundreds of intelligent Miami, Delaware, Shawnee, and Potawatomi who could have offered much more valuable information "than all of the theoretical word-builders on whom the bureau relies can ever furnish." One day, he vowed, the West would finally understand that it had been deprived of its "birthright by a little coterie of perpetual office-holders, and then there will be a time of reckoning."[23]

This "savage and intemperate attack" upon the bureau and its work deeply upset Mooney, who defended his agency in a letter to the editor published in the *Indianapolis News* on 25 April 1907. In addition to attempting to refute charges of mistakes made by the *Handbook of American Indians* as it related to Indiana Native Americans, Mooney took the opportunity, it seems, to disparage Dunn's own work on Indian language. After noting that it took years of arduous study to ready a work of this kind for publication, Mooney stated that no scholar with "a reputation to make or sustain will slight the task for the sake of premature notoriety." He compared the complaints made in the *Star*'s editorial to those made by a princess, "capricious as she was beautiful," who had asked for a bed of seven couches of rose petals. "The couches were finished and laid in place, and the princess slept," Mooney wrote, "but was restless, and in the morning they found that one rose petal in the lowermost couch had been unwittingly crumpled."[24]

Of course, Dunn had to have the last word on the subject. In the *Star*'s editorial pages he admitted that his previous criticism of the bureau might have been a bit too harsh. In its place he offered the story of a mate who had contracted the nautical habit of profanity. This sailor happened to sail with a captain who objected to that sort of language. One day, when the boatswain had failed in his duties, the mate was about to unleash a string of profanities when, at the last moment, he happened to see the captain approaching. Thinking fast, the mate instead shouted, "You naughty, naughty bo's'n!" The *Star*, too, would withdraw its intemperate language, said Dunn, and instead merely say, "'You naughty, naughty bureau!'"[25]

Since Mooney never actually attacks Dunn by name in his letter, it is uncertain if he knew for sure the author of the *Star* editorial. Those in the Indianapolis area, however, were informed of the writer's identity through a small item in the June 1907 edition of the *Indiana Magazine of History*. George S. Cottman, *Indiana Magazine of History* editor, informed the magazine's readers in his "Editorial and Miscellaneous" column of the "interesting and spirited ethnological discussion" printed in the *Star* and *News*. The item also identifies Dunn as the writer of the *Star* editorials. Left unanswered is the question of whether or not the Bureau of

American Ethnology would have retained Dunn's services if it knew that he was the one who had so vigorously attacked the agency's competency.[26]

In spite of his inability to obtain the needed contributions for his society to preserve Indian languages, Dunn continued to do whatever he could to keep alive Native American heritage in the Hoosier State, through writing about the subject for a number of historical journals and by more direct means. At the 1920 Indiana History Conference, sponsored by the Society of Indiana Pioneers in Indianapolis, Harlow Lindley, who chaired the meeting, read to those assembled a communication from the National Research Council, Division of Anthropology and Psychology, calling for the establishment of an archaeological survey in the states of Illinois, Indiana, Iowa, and Missouri. The survey's purpose was to determine "the different types of the remains of the prehistoric population, together with their distribution, so that it may be possible to publish an Archaeological Atlas for each state." The council called on organizations in those states to seek funds for such a study from their legislatures.

Dunn immediately responded to this call for help. He offered a resolution to the conference, which won quick approval, that such a survey should be undertaken by a trained individual under the direction of the Indiana Conservation Commission, today known as the Indiana Department of Natural Resources. Dunn managed to have the history conference appoint a committee of nine people, including himself, to bring the matter to the General Assembly's attention and to "act as a co-operative body with the Conservation Commission and with any similar committees that may be appointed by other organizations to further this work."[27]

Dunn's dedication to preserving the language and customs of Native Americans has not been forgotten. His labor on the Miami language, "to which he devoted so much time, thought, and energy," noted Caroline Dunn, has proven to be, and should continue to be, an invaluable resource for scholars.[28] The work undertaken by Gatschet and Dunn, which has been called "salvage linguistics," has been consulted by historians of the Miami in order to track changes in the group's economic and social life.[29] Dunn's work also anticipated contemporary concerns among linguists and Native Americans over the loss of Indian languages. Responding to these concerns, in 1990 Congress passed the Native American Languages Act, which declared that it was the policy of the United States government to "preserve, protect, and promote the rights and freedom of Native Americans to use, practice, and develop Native American languages."[30] Thanks to Dunn's exertions, the speech of Little Turtle and other noted Hoosier Native Americans has not, as the historian once feared, been consigned to oblivion.

Conclusion

DEFEATED BY THE COURTS IN HIS ATTEMPT TO TRANSFORM INDI-
ana's constitution and unable to find backers for his Miami
language dictionary, Dunn nevertheless continued to immerse himself in Democratic party affairs and historical research. In 1913 he and fellow Hoosier Democrat Maj. G. V.
Menzies of Mount Vernon were under consideration by
President Woodrow Wilson to be named as the United
States minister to Portugal, a job that had been turned
down by Indiana writer and diplomat Meredith Nicholson,
who later served as the American minister to Paraguay,
Venezuela, and Nicaragua during the 1930s and 1940s.
Washington correspondent and Hoosier native Louis Ludlow reported that as a scholar and a literary man, Dunn was
more than capable of filling the post "in accordance with the
highest ideals of the diplomatic service." Also, and perhaps
more important to the Democratic party, the historian's politics had always been of the "regular brand." Another point
in Dunn's favor was his earlier support of the free coinage of
silver, which was looked upon favorably by Secretary of
State William Jennings Bryan, perennial Democratic presidential nominee and a staunch silverite. As Ludlow correctly predicted, however, Indiana lost out on the Portugal
post when Nicholson decided against taking the position.[1]

Instead of a diplomatic berth in Europe, Dunn turned his
attention toward an adventure that would test his historical
detective skills. In December 1921, well into his sixties, he
journeyed to the island of Hispaniola, which includes the

IHS, C7138

Dunn's passport photo before his trip to Haiti

countries of Haiti and the Dominican Republic, with the announced intention of attempting to find the lost gold mine of
Christopher Columbus. "The mine for which Mr. Dunn is
seeking is that from which the gold was taken that was presented to the Spanish court by Columbus on his return from
several of his voyages," according to a page one article on

Dunn's excursion in the *Indianapolis Star*. "Later, apparently following an outbreak among the natives, all trace of the mine was lost."[2]

In this instance Dunn was exercising his well-known wit by spreading such a story. Actually, the main purpose of his journey to the tropics was to prospect for another rich mineral—manganese. For his trip to Hispaniola, the second largest island in the Caribbean, Dunn was acting as field agent for the Hispaniola Mining Company, a group that included as officers such prominent Indianapolis men as Samuel M. Ralston, former Indiana governor; Solomon S. Kiser of the Meyer-Kiser Bank; and Elmer W. Stout of the Fletcher American National Bank. The company charged Dunn with journeying to Hispaniola and, if possible, obtaining a concession for mining manganese under the local laws. Along with a three hundred dollar payment as provision for his family during his absence, those involved in the company placed fifteen hundred dollars in a fund for Dunn to use for expenses on his trip. A cousin of Dunn's wife Charlotte, Edgar Elliott, headed a Haitian-American sugar company and offered Dunn his help in the venture. "From him [Elliott] my father had heard about Haiti, and probably recalled his early silver mining experiences in Colorado," noted Caroline Dunn.[3] Also, Richard Lieber, head of the Indiana Department of Conservation, helped strengthen Dunn's position with United States officials in Haiti (United States military forces occupied Haiti from 1915 to 1934) by appointing him as a special deputy geologist for the collection of exhibits for the Indiana State Museum.[4]

As he had many years before as a prospector in Colorado, Dunn threw himself wholeheartedly into his newest enterprise, frequently writing his family back home in Indianapolis and keeping detailed journals of his experiences. Leaving the United States on 23 December 1921, Dunn journeyed south aboard the Panama Railroad Steamship Line's SS *General Gorgas*, in which he occupied a cabin approximately two feet by six feet in size. The room's small size, and its unfortunate location over some steam pipes, failed to dislodge Dunn's good humor. He noted that his

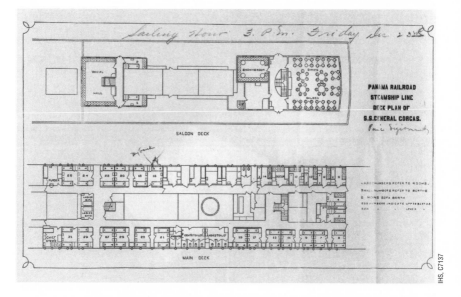

Deck plan of the SS *General Gorgas* with Dunn's penciled notations

quarters were no "worse than a Pullman on the Chesapeake
& Ohio [railroad]."[5]

The sixty-six-year-old Hoosier held up well during the voyage. Dunn confessed in his journals that once or twice during
the first few days onboard he thought he was going to be seasick, but "on taking a little cold water, and sitting on the deck
in the fresh air, it passed off." Talking to the ship's steward
about the matter, Dunn received the advice that seasickness
was mainly "a mental product that if you think about it, and
expect to be sick, you will be." The steward went on to tell
Dunn about one woman passenger who got sick while the
boat was tied to the dock, and not moving at all, becoming
seasick purely from the force of her own imagination.[6]

Onboard the *General Gorgas* Dunn displayed the same
affability he was known for back in the Hoosier State. To
help the passengers become better acquainted, Dunn organized a Christmas Day celebration for the small number of
children on the ship. "There was some difficulty about [ob-
taining] a Santa Claus costume," he noted, "but I made
some whiskers out of a mop furnished by the steward, and
with the aid of a bath robe, a canvas hat, and some rouge, I

got up a fair imitation, or burlesque, of Santa, which satisfied the youngsters." With the cover story that he had arrived by aeroplane, Dunn presented the children with stockings filled with raisins, nuts, and candy. After a quick
costume change, he returned and led the passengers in
rousing versions of such songs as "Tipperary," "My Old Kentucky Home," "Hail, Hail the Gang's All Here," and "How
Dry I Am." The evening's entertainment ended with some
dancing, which shocked Dunn. He wrote that the younger
women danced the most modern dances, including one
called "the wiggle." "I don't understand," Dunn complained,
"how a decent woman can make such an exhibition—am
sure she wouldn't if she could hear how the men talked
about it."[7]

Arriving in Port-au-Prince on 29 December 1921, Dunn
had to fend off a hoard of begging Haitian youths and sou-
venir sellers peddling their wares to arriving tourists. Set-
tling in at lodgings provided by the Haytian American Sugar
Company (known in Haiti as Hasco), the firm that employed
his wife's cousin, Dunn had time to survey his surroundings
and the social scene. "I really feel sorry for the white women
here," he wrote his daughter Eleanor, "they have such a hard
time to amuse themselves. It hardly pays to be domestic, because you can hire five servants here for what you pay one at
home, and there is hardly any form of amusement but riding
and playing cards and dancing." Although at first this might
not have seemed so bad a life, Dunn told his daughter that
the married women were not "eagerly sought as partners at
dances." Instead, the younger American men in the country
were "more inclined to seek the Haitian dances, where the
ladies are somewhat darker, but at least younger."[8]

Along with casting his historian's eye on the social scene,
Dunn was able during the next few days to prepare himself
for his mineral exploration of Haiti. Before journeying into
the countryside he consulted with Prof. Edward Roumain,
who was in charge of Haiti's exhibit at the 1904 St. Louis
Exposition. "I am convinced," Dunn confided in his log, "that
he [Roumain] was the only man on the island who knew
about minerals." Roumain welcomed the Hoosier explorer

"with open arms" and promised to help Dunn find a guide for his trip. After conferring with Roumain, Dunn next busied himself with purchasing his supplies. He bought a horse, complete with saddle and bridle, for thirty-six dollars and also furnished himself with a pickax, frying pan, small stew pan, two teaspoons, two tin cups, two small cans of Armour pork and beans, and three cans of sardines. Also, on the advice of American officials worried that Dunn might be set upon by thieves during his journey, he received permission from Haiti's chief of police to carry a 44-caliber Colt revolver, serial number 264804, and twenty rounds of ammunition.[9]

For a man well into his sixties, Dunn was embarking on a truly strenuous endeavor as Haiti is more mountainous than even Switzerland. One story about the country has an English admiral crumpling a sheet of paper, placing it on a table, and remarking to King George III: "Sire, Haiti looks like that."[10] For his ambitious trip into the Haitian interior, Dunn hired a guide named Oceant Noël, a bespectacled black man he described as being only four feet, six inches tall. Noël agreed to be Dunn's guide for five days, furnish his own horse, a pack animal, and an interpreter, all for twenty-nine dollars. The interpreter, named Salomon Télamour, "proved to have command of about thirty words of English, but is quite proud of them," Dunn said. Leaving Port-au-Prince on 9 January 1922 (Dunn complained throughout his stay of the often lax attitude his guides took about being on time), the three men attracted quite a bit of attention from Haitians. "I was clad in khaki shirt and pants," said Dunn, "with leggings, and my artillery swung on a belt." Noël, the guide, wore a black coat, Panama hat, and spectacles. "He would have passed for an A.M.E. preacher in the States," Dunn noted. The interpreter, Télamour, was described by the American as "the dude of the party," as he wore a two-piece suit of light colored material with a dark stripe, white canvas shoes, and a Panama hat. Télamour provided a bit of comic relief by riding on top of the packhorse. His legs "stuck out at angles of about 45 degrees, and were in constant motion, as were also his arms," Dunn commented in his log of the trip. "He carried a stick with which he belabored his [horse] and also cheered it by yelling 'Kurrk'—or something that sounded that way. Most of these people talk to their horses . . . just as they would to a person."[11]

The descriptions of this small band of explorers particularly tickled the fancy of Charlotte Dunn, who wrote her husband that it seemed to her "that you and your retinue, when you start out prospecting, must look not unlike Don Quixote and his Sancho Panza! Your dun-colored steed and your long, thin legs! But I hope you may have all the good luck you desire, as well as the adventure." Charlotte was so taken with the Don Quixote image that she addressed later letters to her husband as "My Dear Don Quixote."[12]

The elderly Dunn managed to make his excursions into the mountainous countryside without too much difficulty. The local food did upset his "internal workings," which he later calmed with liberal doses of milk of magnesia, and when arising in the morning after trying to sleep on a hammock (the cold night air kept him awake), he had to "do gymnastics for several minutes" in order to relieve his cramped muscles. Although his companions claimed he spoke the native French "like a French oyster," Dunn was able to build good relations with the Haitians he encountered on his travels due to tendering a "substantial [monetary] reward for any service rendered."[13]

"Altogether they [the Haitians] are as child-like a lot—when far from foreign contact—as could be imagined," Dunn said. "They are all Catholic, and most of them go to church in the morning but are said to attend voodoo dances at night. . . . I ran across little chapels and establishments of various Catholic orders at numerous out-of-the-way places." The Haitians were often drawn to Catholicism, said Dunn, because they believed that the church had "magic" superior to voodoo priests and priestesses. A Catholic priest in Haiti told Dunn about a young Haitian woman who asked her priest for a Bible even though she could not read. "He finally gave her one, and a few weeks later was appalled to learn that she had been eating a page of it every day," Dunn recalled. "Her idea was to get the 'magic' in concentrated form."[14]

Dunn may have had good luck in charming the native Haitians with his largesse, but he failed in his quest to discover sufficient quantities of manganese to risk large-scale mining operations in the country. Returning with his specimens to Port-au-Prince on 17 January 1922, Dunn had his first bath and shave in almost a week. His adventure, it seems, had taken a toll. "Appearance somewhat improved," he noted in his log, "but a trifle gaunt. The trip had evidently been some strain." Refreshed, Dunn took the specimens he collected to be analyzed at the sugar company's laboratory by a Doctor Joy, a Haitian chemist employed by the firm. "We satisfied ourselves," Dunn said, "that there was not a particle of manganese in any of them." He later wrote his wife the following about his unfortunate news: "I am including the log herewith, and there is little else to say. The manganese scheme is gone glimmering, and I expect to know pretty soon whether there is anything in the gold proposition."[15]

Coming up empty in Haiti, Dunn hoped for better luck in the neighboring Santo Domingo, which since 1916 had been occupied by United States Marines. "There is a striking contrast between Port au Prince and this place—all in favor of Santo Domingo, which is quite up to date in appearance, though it has no street railways, no street lighting, and a very poor water supply," Dunn wrote upon arriving in Santo Domingo on 30 January 1922. "The people are generally well dressed, and a surprising number of them speak English more or less—commonly less."[16]

While in Santo Domingo, Dunn conferred with United States officials in charge of public works for the country and was able to obtain motor transportation into the countryside where he could investigate reports of large manganese and gold deposits. He left Santo Domingo on 8 February 1922 and established a base at a garage and repair shop run by Americans in charge of repairing and refurbishing the road system. Shown to a spring bed on which he was to sleep that first night, Dunn ruefully noted that his "last

[—] of 'roughing it' are gone." Although his guides for his prospecting trip spoke no English, Dunn managed to make himself understood and tramped through the mountains searching for the riches he had been led to believe were there for the taking; it was all for naught. His journal reflected his bitter disappointment: "Strenuous day. . . . I finally got to the place at 1:30, and by the time I had taken a look at it, and eaten lunch it was 2:30. It is no good."[17] Charlotte Dunn sympathized with her husband's misfortune, writing: "Too bad about the manganese. I hope other things will look more promising—but you know I was never very optimistic. Still, success would be most welcome! At any rate, you are getting this out of your system, and having a complete change and a good time. Perhaps something good will 'turn up' when you return."[18]

A disappointed Dunn returned to the United States the same way he had gone: by boat. As with the trip south, the voyage north proved to be a fine opportunity for Dunn to enlarge his circle of acquaintances. "The men on the boat are most Americans and are a thoroughly argumentative outfit," he noted. "We have discussed and disposed of a large number of questions already." Unlucky at prospecting, Dunn found he had better luck at cards, winning a reputation as a "card sharp" for his skill at pinochle, where he won the princely sum of thirty-six cents during one high stakes game. The only sour note on his return home was struck by an Irish lady who recommended that Dunn read an editorial in the *Smart Set* by H. L. Mencken. "It was rotten stuff," said Dunn, "and she was very much disgusted with my lack of appreciation—observed that I might be 'one of them boobs that believe in prohibition and that sort of stuff.'"[19]

The Hoosier historian arrived back in New York Harbor on 2 March 1922 and made his way overland to his Indianapolis home. His bold adventure in the West Indies may have failed to provide Dunn with riches from precious metals, but it did offer him the opportunity to investigate and write about Haitian dialects and the island's voodoo cult for Indianapolis newspapers.[20] Dunn wrote a particularly lively series of articles engaging in a battle of words with

Ernest H. Gruening, *The Nation* managing editor, over an article Gruening penned for the periodical *Current History* discussing the American occupation of Haiti and Santo Domingo. Dunn believed that Gruening's article had besmirched the reputation of the United States Marines, and he attempted to set the record straight in articles for the *Indianapolis News*. After all, he added, before Gruening's piece of "propaganda of defamation," *Current History* had established a reputation for reliability. "Getting misinformation from it," Dunn said, "is like getting poisoned food from a trusted friend." Gruening personally challenged his Indianapolis foe "to prove a single misstatement of fact" in his story.[21]

This was a chance too good for a man with Dunn's instinct for the editorial jugular to ignore. He set out to slice into pieces Gruening's work with the same fiery spirit he displayed in earlier days lambasting wayward Democrats. In particular, he jumped on a statement by Gruening that after the death of Charlemagne Péralte, a Haitian chief who opposed American forces, his followers were "rapidly exterminated." In fact, Dunn pointed out that these followers, 2,995 in one month and more than 10,000 from 27 December 1919 to 10 March 1920, had taken advantage of an amnesty program offered by American military officials. "Just consider the outrage!" Dunn wrote. "In ten weeks more than four times as many Haitian patriots as had been killed in five and one-half years, actually wiped out and converted into 'good citizens' by this fiendish device of the oppressors. And Mr. Gruening asks for proof of 'one misstatement of fact.' Does the man want the earth?"[22]

In another article for the *Indianapolis News*, Dunn claimed that under American rule the Dominican people had "prospered as never before." He noted that imports to the country had grown from $11,664,430 in 1916 to $46,525,376 in 1920, plus a nearly eight million dollar increase in exports from 1916 to 1919. Also, he pointed to the various public improvements made by the United States— roads, docks, harbors, lighthouses, schools, and public buildings. "The American administration has made more public improvements since 1916 than the Dominicans had made in a century," Dunn said.[23]

Engaging in such newspaper skirmishes might have provided a way for Dunn to salve an ego bruised a bit by returning from the West Indies empty-handed, but a far greater chance to redeem himself beckoned a year after his Haitian experience. Newly elected United States senator Samuel M. Ralston, former Indiana governor, selected Dunn to be his private secretary for his Washington office. Before this appointment the two men had enjoyed very cordial relations, with Dunn serving as an adviser to Ralston on public policy issues and Ralston was a business partner in Dunn's unsuccessful search for minerals in Hispaniola. In offering his advice during Ralston's governorship, Dunn, the veteran of many political wars and one who was unafraid to state his opinion on any subject, counseled Ralston to take the same direct approach. On the matter of Ralston's position, for example, on the National Prohibition Enforcement

IHS, Bass Photo Collection, 41510

Indiana governor and United States senator Samuel M. Ralston

Act, passed in 1920 and more commonly known as the Volstead Act, Dunn advised Ralston to "'go the whole hog'" on the issue and take a solid position supporting prohibition. To Dunn's way of thinking, there existed no middle ground on "this question that will satisfy people who are really interested on either side, and if you are going to lose one crowd you can profitably gain the other."[24]

In his letters back home to his daughter Caroline in Indianapolis, Dunn seemed to be enjoying life in the nation's capital, commenting in his letters on politics and society, including the funeral of former president Woodrow Wilson. Although many in Washington were disappointed that Edith Wilson declined a state funeral for her husband, Dunn supported her actions, telling his daughter that he suspected Mrs. Wilson did not want "to accept any hypocritical favors from the bunch that hunted Wilson down." He compared the situation to what happened when Theodore Roosevelt died and "all the Republican standpatters discovered what a wonderful man he was, and fell over each other mourning him, although they had laid awake hating him before his death."[25]

In other letters Dunn informed his family that the burdens of his office were few and far between. "The worst task," Dunn said, "is listening to people talk when you would like to throw them out, but know that you have to be moderately polite." The historian turned bureaucrat did go on to say that many persons came into Ralston's Senate office who were "sources of pleasure, so that it balances up fairly well."[26]

Dunn's time in the nation's capital, however, was short. During his travels in Haiti he had contracted some form of tropical disease that left him susceptible to jaundice. His ill health forced his return to Indianapolis where he died on 6 June 1924. Dunn's death was front-page news in both the *Indianapolis Star* and *Indianapolis News*. Commenting on his fellow Democrat's death, Ralston expressed his "great admiration" for Dunn. Ralston noted that the first time he heard Dunn make a speech his subject was the value of circulating libraries to citizens. "It was characteristic of him to be most interested in those things that most benefited the people," said Ralston. "He could become as indignant as any man I ever knew at the failure of a public official to perform his duties." He was not only loyal to the truth, at whatever the cost, the United States senator continued, but also loyal to his friends. "And trustworthy—absolutely so," said Ralston. "I shall miss him."[27]

An editorial in the *Indianapolis News* commented that it would seem strange to wander through the streets in the city with Dunn absent from the scene. "His acquaintance was large, and he was a welcome guest in any company because of his superior knowledge and his capacity for witty observations," the *News* said. "He was a dreaded foe to sham and to complacent acceptance of long standing and unexamined theories." When the history of Dunn's time was written, the newspaper predicted, his name "is destined to a distinct place in Indiana history and literature. Personally, too, he will be greatly missed. He was individual and distinctive, admired for his intellectual qualities and loved for his genial companionship."[28]

Dunn's place in the history of Indiana and Indianapolis is secure. But there have been some who expressed regret that Dunn had not been born into a family of great wealth and prominence so he could have become Indiana's version of nationally prominent historian-politicians such as Henry Cabot Lodge and Theodore Roosevelt, or as Henry Adams who pursued a doctorate in history so that his researches into the past might have received the support and encouragement of an academic setting.[29] Dunn's work on local and state history, however, has weathered the years far better than many others, especially his book *Greater Indianapolis*, which has served as *the* standard work on the Hoosier capital's history for more than eighty years and is still consulted today by students and scholars interested in the city's early development. Also, as an often active participant in Indianapolis's civic affairs through his career in journalism and politics, Dunn, more so perhaps than a historian merely consulting paper documents, had the ability to impart to his readers the "inside story" of some of the events that helped to shape the community.

Often openly partisan in his support of the Democratic party, something he would be the first to admit, Dunn still proved to be scrupulous in presenting both sides of an issue. He may have questioned the correctness of a particular opposition politician's position on a point under debate, but Dunn recorded for posterity's sake all the details of that person's argument. Following his repudiation at the polls by British voters in 1945, Prime Minister Winston Churchill commented that for his part he considered it "will be found much better by all parties to leave the past to history, especially as I propose to write that history myself."[30] Dunn, too, possessed this ability. No matter if he or his party were beaten on a particular issue, he took some satisfaction in knowing that he could always have the last word on an issue through his writings.

Along with fellow amateurs John B. Dillon and George S. Cottman, Dunn stands as one of the leading figures in Indiana's early historiography. Dunn also deserves, however, a foremost spot in the Hoosier State's political history for his efforts on behalf of numerous reform measures during the late nineteenth and early twentieth centuries, especially his crusades to purify the ballot in Indiana. This blending of history and politics seemed a natural affair to Dunn who believed that "a state can not possibly profit fully by its experience unless it provides for handing it down from one generation to another by the preservation of its history."[31] Through his personal involvement in issues and his writing about them, Dunn made certain that no Hoosier would soon forget the lessons of his time.

Appendix

THE FOLLOWING ARE TRANSCRIBED ENTRIES FROM THE LOGS DUNN KEPT AND sent to his family in Indianapolis and are located in the manuscript collections of the Indiana Historical Society Library. They describe his experiences prospecting for manganese in the West Indies at the ripe old age of sixty-six. This sample begins with Dunn's adventures on board the SS *General Gorgas* on his voyage to Haiti and reflects the excitement and anticipation Dunn felt at the time—almost as if he were a young man again hoping to strike it rich in the Colorado gold and silver fields. It ends with his early explorations of the Haitian countryside.

Dec. 25. Christmas Day broke in a dream of beauty. The sunrise was lovely. The wind had gone down, and the sea had become smooth—at least in comparison with what it had been. The air was balmy. I began the day by taking a cold, sea-water shower bath, and substituting b.v.d's for my heavy underclothes.

I scraped up an acquaintance yesterday with a youngster who was not feeling well, and had been packed up on a steamer-chair to get the air. She was the daughter of the manager of the street fair outfit [headed to Panama for a performance], and is a very bright kid. I asked her what made the white (foam) on the water, and she said it was soap-suds coming up from below. I suggested that maybe the fish had a laundry under the water, and she thought it a possible explanation. I then inquired where the blue came from, and she was dubious. I told her that I thought it came from the wind—that when the wind blew the blue came off and got into the water. She gave this scant consideration, announcing that it could not be done. She said it came from the starch, and when I insisted that starch was white she said they had blue starch at their house. (Her mother informed me that she was accustomed to put blueing in the starch.) Then she told me about Santa Claus, and fairies and angels, especially about the wings of the last two—what they were made of and how they were fastened on.

It struck me that we ought to have some Christmas celebration, as the passengers had not got acquainted much, and there were two little boys, about Annette's age [Annette was the aforementioned young girl], and no other children but one baby. I suggested it to several, and everybody fell in, especially the women. So we decided—or at least I did—on a social entertainment after supper, in the "Social Room," which is a large cabin at the stern serving as a sort of ladies parlor. It has a piano which looks like it had been through the war, but sounds fairly well.

The youngest Miss Duque (this is Spanish, and pronounced Du' Ky) played the piano, and one of the fair crowd, named Davenport, was very good on the violin. I got them together and practiced up on popular songs. There was some difficulty about a Santa Claus costume, but I made some whiskers out of a mop furnished by the steward, and with the aid of a bath robe, a canvas hat, and some rouge, I got up a fair imitation, or burlesque, of Santa, which satisfied the youngsters. Annette was rather dubious at first as the costume was short on fur, and the whiskers were rather long; but her mother explained that I had to put on summer clothes on account of the warmth, and she accepted me.

We started out with some records—young Duque had a phonograph —and then the master of ceremonies (Mr. Rubens, of the fair outfit) announced that Santa Claus had just arrived by aeroplane. I entered, and was received with great hilarity. I announced that I had learned there were three children on board, but that I had been unable to find them because they did not hang up their stockings; and I had been hunting all over the world for them. Junior Shoemaker, one of the boys (they call him Junior because he was named for his father) at once piped up that his Mama had told him there was no use of hanging it up on the ship, and he was not to blame. This brought down the house, and Homer Mumy hastened to explain that he did not hang his up because he couldn't find any place to hang it. I had got a stocking of each from their mothers, and filled them with raisins, nuts, and candy; and after presenting these to them I explained that I had to get back to New York where I had left my sleigh and reindeer because there was no snow south of there. The three kids rushed forward and shook hands, and thanked me, and I hustled off to the aeroplane.

When I came back we opened up with "Tipperary" following with "Old Kentucky Home" "Hail! Hail The Gang's all here," "How dry I am," "Katy," "Mother Machree," "Adaline," "Daddy" etc. Then they danced a while . . . not more than a dozen danced at all, and the younger ones did the most modern stuff, including "the wiggle." I dont understand how a decent woman can make such an exhibition—am sure she wouldn't if she could hear how the men talked about it. We wound up with "America" and the national air of Columbia; and everybody pronounced the affair a great success.

Jan. 9. Our 6 a.m. departure . . . was not on schedule time. If there is any respect in which the Haitian is not late I have not struck it. Breakfast was to be ready, and my horse at the door at 5:30. At that hour the dining-room and kitchen was locked, and defied my efforts to get in. One of the men arrived just before 6, and with his aid I broke in and got some fruit, bread, butter, cold ham and a cup of coffee; after which I carried my saddle bags down to the stable, and found the horse not ready. I was getting pretty warm, but reflected that Oceant had been late for two days and would suffer just retribution by waiting for me.

I rode across the city [Port-au-Prince], purchasing some bread and other things on the way. The only store where I could buy American smoking tobacco was not open—I was out of it, and Haitian tobacco is deadly. Luckily, while in despair, Major Rupertis [an American officer] came up in his auto, and, on learning the situation, donated a box of Prince Albert. I was then all set except that my money was in American bills; but I got a man at a Dodge auto agency to give me Haitian [money] for $15, after some kicking because his case was made up for deposit. I did not worry about that because I knew that the consciousness of a good deed would repay him in his old age.

It was almost 8 when I got to Roumains [an employee of the sugar company where Dunn had been staying]—and Oceant and Salomon had not arrived. Roumain was dancing a war dance; but they showed up a few minutes later. Then there was more delay while Roumain gave final instructions on all subjects to everybody—he ran after us for a half a-block to say something he had overlooked—and finally we were off.

It was pleasant for about an hour. The Leogane road, which we followed, is one of the roads the Americans have improved. It was along the south shore of the great bay that separates the two western arms of Haiti, much of the way within a few feet of the beach—or shore, which is more swamp than beach. The road was much like the road to Hasco [the Haytian American Sugar Company] in its streams of travel on foot, donkey and horse, with an occasional auto, but there were more signs of diversified industry. It was all strikingly like our early French customs. The bull-carts are great lumbering things with wheels that look like they would come off or break down at any moment. The bulls are yoked by their horns instead of on their necks. All the lumber I saw being transported by Haitians was carried on the head, usually by one man, with the boards balanced in the middle, but occasionally by two—one on each end.

I passed two or three "ship-yards," where sloops 20 or 30 feet long were in various stages of construction, but in only one did the work appear to be in progress. I feel confident that these boats were being built exactly as La Salle built "The Griffen." It made it easy to understand how shipwrecked explorers, and buccaneers, built the boats on which they sailed.

After the first hour the ride was hot and tiresome, with no available drinking water—it has not rained a drop since I have been on the island.

I was much relieved when we reached Flon where is located the Hasco sugar plantation at which Montigue and Riess are located. They received me with open arms, and I had a very restful hour, and a good dinner. The house in which they live is a delightful old French structure, two-stories in hight, with a massive stone stairway, on the outside, to the second floor. I christened it "Castle Montigue."

The "old Jacmel road" leaves the Leogane road at this point. I think Flon (pronounced almost like Fï-lon) is not marked on the map I sent you. It is about 4 miles east of Leogane, and was formerly called "Momance."

Our party unquestionably attracted attention on the road. I was clad in khaki shirt and pants, with leggings, and my artillery swung on a belt. I heard "gens d'amie" several times from spectators. Oceant wore a black coat, Panama hat, and spectacles. He would have passed for an A.M.E. preacher in the States. Salomon was the dude of the party. He wore a two-piece suit of light colored material, with a dark stripe, white canvas shoes and a Panama hat. I thought my horse was small, but his was only about half as large, and carried the packs—Salomon riding on top. In consequence his legs stuck out at angles of about 45 degrees, and were in constant motion, as were also his arms. He carried a stick with which he belabored his [horse] and also cheered it by yelling "Kurrk"—or something that sounded that way. Most of these people [the Haitians] talk to their horses . . . just as they would to a person.

After leaving Flon, we traveled through vast fields of sugar-cane, and then through banana plantations. It seemed as if there were enough banana trees to supply the world. By the way they call a banana a "fig" here, and a "banana" is a plantain, which is the size and shape of a banana, but always green in color, and must be cooked to be eaten. I tried one boiled, and it tasted something like a cross between a potato and a carrot.

We struck the foot-hills after passing the bananas, and cultivation became only occasional for lack of irrigation facilities. It was pretty stiff climbing, and it seemed to me we crossed two or three ridges, from the first of which there was a magnificent view of the whole Leogane plain. The sun was about to set when we reached what Oceant called the "sommet," and it was dark a few minutes later; but fortunately the moon was near full, for it was a good hour later when we reached the "caille" of Oceant's cousin, M. Blansi, where we stopped for the night.

It was the ordinary Haitian hut, but with a sort of portico over which there was a thatched roof. I swung my hammock between two posts of the portico. It felt very comfortable when I got in, but it got so cold in the night that I could not sleep well, and I could not get into any position but on my back, curved up like a new moon. In the morning my legs were so cramped that I had to do gymnastics for several minutes before attaining normalcy.

I found here a slight aid in language. M. Blansi's daughter, Julienne, informed me that she "worked for the Cor-o-nel's wife at Port au Prince, and went on a trip with her to New York, where she acquired English." She did not know what the Coronel's last name was; and her English vocabulary was brief, even for New York. However, her 20 words were not the same as Salomon's, and every little [bit] helped at odd times. Mme. Blansi was quite elderly, but very active. She did the cooking—in a little shack near the caille, as is the Haitian custom—and was somewhat put out when I cooked some pork and beans (Armour's) for myself. However, she was gratified when I took some of her ca-fe, which was not quite so thick and muddy as the ordinary Haitian make; and was quite delighted when I gave her . . . 10 cob on leaving. I had obtained about five pounds of Haitian coin on starting, and I found it good policy to give the kids a 5-cob "bon" and also to tender some equally substantial reward for any service rendered.

Notes

Note to Preface

1. Barbara W. Tuchman, *Practicing History* (New York: Ballantine Books, 1982), 35.

Notes to Introduction

1. Frederick M. Davenport, "The Pre-Nomination Campaign: The Light Breaking over Stand-Pat Indiana," *The Outlook* (24 May 1916): 177.

2. As quoted in David Turpie, *Sketches of My Own Times* (Indianapolis: Bobbs-Merrill Co., 1903), 302–3.

3. Clifton J. Phillips, *Indiana in Transition: The Emergence of an Industrial Commonwealth, 1880–1920* (Indianapolis: Indiana Historical Bureau and Indiana Historical Society, 1968), 2. See also Ralph D. Gray, *Indiana's Favorite Sons, 1840–1940* (Indianapolis: Indiana Historical Society, 1988), 6–7; Melvyn Hammarberg, *The Indiana Voter: The Historical Dynamics of Party Allegiance during the 1870s* (Chicago: The University of Chicago Press, 1977), 18–19; and Philip R. VanderMeer, *The Hoosier Politician: Officeholding and Political Culture in Indiana, 1896–1920* (Urbana: University of Illinois Press, 1985), 11–12.

4. Jacob Piatt Dunn, Jr., *Greater Indianapolis: The History, the Industries, the Institutions, and the People of a City of Homes*, 2 vols. (Chicago: The Lewis Publishing Co., 1910), 1:292–94.

5. William P. Fishback, *A Plea for Honest Elections: An Address Delivered to the Students of the Indiana State University, May, 1886* (Indianapolis: A. R. Baker, Printer, 1886), 17–18.

6. Dunn, *Greater Indianapolis*, 1:292–94. Despite his lifelong attempt to cleanse the sordid mess at Indiana's ballot box, Dunn possessed a grudging respect for those involved with besmirching the state's reputation. One of these characters was Simeon Coy, Marion County Democratic party chairman and city council representative for the Eighteenth Ward. Reputed to be the illegitimate son of a prominent

Indianapolis businessman, Coy worked his way up from serving as an apprentice printer to becoming the "absolute dictator in Marion county politics," according to the *Indianapolis News*.

"He [Coy] had no scruples about political crookedness. That was part of 'the game,' as played by nine-tenths of those in it; and the man who did not take any kind of political advantage when he had the opportunity was not only a 'chump,' but was not 'playing the game,'" Dunn said. Although he thought of Coy as a crook, Dunn acknowledged that the Democratic boss, who went to jail for altering tally sheets in the 1886 Indianapolis city elections for criminal court judge, did have in him a form of honesty. "It was universally conceded that if he were given money to 'buy a crowd,' he either accomplished the result or returned the money," said Dunn. Coy's supreme contempt, the historian went on to say, was for the man "'who wouldn't stay bought when he was bought.'" After serving his sentence in the Michigan City prison, Coy came back to Indianapolis and regained his old city council seat. Dunn, *Greater Indianapolis*, 1:294. See also William Dudley Foulke, *Marion County, Indiana, Tally Sheet Forgeries: Speech Delivered by Hon. W. D. Foulke* (Indianapolis: n.p., n.d.); Phillips, *Indiana in Transition*, 28; and *Indianapolis News*, 23 Sept. 1913. For Coy's entertaining version of the tally sheet case, see Simeon Coy, *The Great Conspiracy: A Complete History of the Famous Tally-Sheet Cases* (Indianapolis: n.p., 1889).

7. *Opening Speech of J. P. Dunn, Democratic Candidate for Congress in the Seventh Indiana Congressional District, Delivered at Masonic Hall, Indianapolis, October 2, 1902* (Indianapolis: Allied Printing, [1902]), 14.

8. Taken from biographical sketch of Judge Isaac Blackford, pp. 22, 25, box 1, folder 2, Jacob Piatt Dunn, Jr., Papers, Indiana State Library, Indiana Division, Indianapolis (hereafter cited as Dunn Papers, ISL).

9. Keith W. Olson, *Biography of a Progressive: Franklin K. Lane, 1864–1921* (Westport, Conn.: Greenwood Press, 1979), 5–6. See also Arthur S. Link and Richard L. McCormick, *Progressivism* (Arlington Heights, Ill.: Harlan Davidson, 1983), and Daniel T. Rodgers, "In Search of Progressivism," *Reviews in American History* 10, no. 4 (Dec. 1982): 113–32.

10. Russel B. Nye, *Midwestern Progressive Politics: A Historical Study of Its Origins and Development, 1870–1958* (East Lansing: Michigan State University Press, 1959), 186.

11. Untitled speech on suffrage, Dunn Papers, ISL.

12. Richard L. McCormick, *The Party Period and Public Policy: American Politics from the Age of Jackson to the Progressive Era* (New York: Oxford University Press, 1986), 228–29.

13. Richard J. Jensen, *The Winning of the Midwest: Social and Political Conflict, 1888–1896* (Chicago: The University of Chicago Press, 1971), 6–7. See also Michael E. McGerr, *The Decline of Popular Politics:*

The American North, 1865–1928 (New York: Oxford University Press, 1986), 12–14. VanderMeer notes that not only was party identification widespread during this period, it was also very public in nature. "Newspapers commonly noted a person's affiliation, and biographical sketches in the inumerable collections published in the late nineteenth and early twentieth centuries invariably mentioned party ties." See VanderMeer, *The Hoosier Politician*, 24–25.

14. Caroline Dunn, *Jacob Piatt Dunn: His Miami Language Studies and Indian Manuscript Collection, Prehistory Research Series*, vol. 1, no. 2 (Indianapolis: Indiana Historical Society, 1937), 32–35.

15. Jacob Piatt Dunn, "Duty of the State to Its History," *Indiana Magazine of History* 6 (Dec. 1910): 137–38.

16. Ibid., 138.

17. Jacob Piatt Dunn, "Shall Indian Languages Be Preserved?," *Journal of the Illinois State Historical Society* 10 (Apr. 1917): 87.

18. *Opening Speech of J. P. Dunn*, 3.

19. Jacob Piatt Dunn, *The New Tax Law of Indiana and the Science of Taxation* (Indianapolis: Indianapolis Printing Co., 1892), 35–36; *The Omitted Paper: Municipal Financial Pressure, an Address before the Second Annual Conference on Taxation in Indiana by J. P. Dunn, City Controller of Indianapolis* (Indianapolis: Premier Printing Co., 1914), 1; and *The Real Trouble with the Indiana Tax Law: An Address by J. P. Dunn, City Controller of Indianapolis, at the Bloomington Tax Conference, February 5 and 6, 1914* (n.p., 1914), 8.

20. Richard Hofstadter, *The Age of Reform: From Bryan to F. D. R.* (New York: Vintage Books, 1955), 203.

21. Jacob Piatt Dunn, *Why Is a Democrat? Speech of Hon. Jacob P. Dunn on the Issues of the Present City Campaign, before the Democratic Business Men's Meeting at the Denison Hotel, September 26, 1913* (Indianapolis: n.p., n.d.), 3.

22. William L. Riordon, comp., *Plunkitt of Tammany Hall: A Series of Very Plain Talks on Very Practical Politics, Delivered by Ex-Senator George Washington Plunkitt, the Tammany Philosopher, from His Rostrum—The New York County Court House Bootblack Stand* (New York: E. P. Dutton, 1963), 17.

23. Dunn, *Why Is a Democrat?*, 5.

24. Jacob Piatt Dunn, *Indiana and Indianans: A History of Aboriginal and Territorial Indiana and the Century of Statehood*, 5 vols. (Chicago and New York: The American Historical Society, 1919), 2:747.

25. William J. Crotty, *Political Reform and the American Experiment* (New York: Thomas Y. Crowell Co., 1977), 4. See also Frances Fox Piven and Richard A. Cloward, *Why Americans Don't Vote* (New York: Pantheon Books, 1989).

26. Jacob Piatt Dunn, *The Proposed Constitution of Indiana* (Indianapolis: Sentinel Printing Co., 1911), 30.

27. Jacob Piatt Dunn, *The Negro Issue: An Address by Jacob Piatt Dunn, City Controller of Indianapolis, before the Indiana Democratic Club, October 13, 1904* (Indianapolis: Sentinel Printing Co., 1904), 17, 22. See also *Indianapolis News*, 14 Oct. 1904.

28. Talk titled "Walam Olum" in Caroline Dunn Papers, Indiana Historical Society Library, Indianapolis.

29. See James A. Woodburn, *The Indiana Historical Society: A Hundred Years,* Indiana Historical Society *Publications,* vol. 10 (Indianapolis: The Bobbs-Merrill Co., 1933), 27.

30. Rodgers, "In Search of Progressivism," 122.

Notes to Chapter 1

1. *Indianapolis News*, 7 June 1924.

2. John H. B. Nowland, *Sketches of Prominent Citizens of 1876: With a Few of the Pioneers of the City and County Who Have Passed Away* (Indianapolis: Tilford and Carlon, Printers, 1877), 553–54.

3. "Jacob Piatt Dunn, Senior," Citizens Historical Association, Newspaper Clipping File, Indiana Division, Indiana State Library, Indianapolis.

4. Jacob Piatt Dunn Papers, Indiana Historical Society Library, Indianapolis (hereafter cited as Dunn Papers, IHS). Dunn remained a highly religious man throughout his life. In 1914 he published a book that included an essay on "The Passing of Darwinism." The piece attacked Charles Darwin's theory of evolution as "the most tremendous air-bubble of all the ages." He confidently states that Darwin's ideas on natural selection "stand today seriously discredited in the biological world." Dunn, *The Unknown God and Other Orthodox Essays* (Indianapolis: Sentinel Printing Co., 1914), 98, 110.

5. *Year Book of the Society of Indiana Pioneers, 1922* (n.p., 1922), 10.

6. Ibid.

7. Robert Morse Crunden, *Ministers of Reform: The Progressives' Achievement in American Civilization, 1889–1920* (New York: Basic Books, 1982), ix. Much of the Progressive movement had an "evangelical ethos," one that worked within the "modern citadels of sin"—the crowded industrial cities of the country. See Richard L. McCormick, *The Party Period and Public Policy: American Politics from the Age of Jackson to the Progressive Era* (New York: Oxford University Press, 1986), 271.

8. *Indianapolis Star*, 7 June 1924.

9. Opal Thornburg, *Earlham: The Story of the College, 1847–1962* (Richmond, Ind.: The Earlham College Press, 1963), 73.

10. Ibid., 130.

11. Jacob Piatt Dunn, "The Origin of the Earlhamite," *The Earlhamite* 21 (June 1894): 137–38. See also "The Record of Twenty-One Years" in that same issue.

12. Dunn, "The Origin of the Earlhamite," 137–38.

13. Jacob Piatt Dunn, "Trip to the Mammoth Cave," *The Earlhamite* 3 (Jan. 1876): 64.

14. Jacob Piatt Dunn, "Reform in Spelling," ibid. 8 (Apr. 1881): 154.

15. John M. Butler to Lew Wallace, 11 Mar. 1879, box 2, folder 7, Dunn Papers, IHS.

16. Newspaper clipping, 31 Mar. 1879, scrapbook, ibid.

17. Carl Ubbelohde, Maxine Benson, and Duane A. Smith, eds., *A Colorado History,* 5th ed. (Boulder, Colo.: Pruett Publishing Co., 1982), 162–63.

18. Newspaper clipping, 31 Mar. 1879, scrapbook, Dunn Papers, IHS.

19. Correspondence from Jacob Piatt Dunn to the *Indianapolis Saturday Herald,* 4 July 1879, ibid.

20. Ibid.

21. For information on Dunn's life, see Ray Boomhower, "'To Secure Honest Elections': Jacob Piatt Dunn, Jr., and the Reform of Indiana's Ballot," *Indiana Magazine of History* 90 (Dec. 1994): 311–45; Caroline Dunn, *Jacob Piatt Dunn: His Miami Language Studies and Indian Manuscript Collection, Prehistory Research Series,* vol. 1, no. 2 (Indianapolis: Indiana Historical Society, 1937); Jacob Piatt Dunn, Jr., *Greater Indianapolis: The History, the Industries, the Institutions, and the People of a City of Homes,* 2 vols. (Chicago: The Lewis Publishing Co., 1910), 2:1255–57, and *Indiana and Indianans: A History of Aboriginal and Territorial Indiana and the Century of Statehood,* 5 vols. (Chicago and New York: The American Historical Society, 1919), 5:2290–91; Lana Ruegamer, *A History of the Indiana Historical Society, 1830–1980* (Indianapolis: Indiana Historical Society, 1980), chapters 3 and 4, and "History, Politics, and the Active Life: Jacob Piatt Dunn, Progressive Historian," *Indiana Magazine of History* 81 (Sept. 1985): 265–83; "Jacob Piatt Dunn," *Indiana History Bulletin* 1 (Aug. 1924): 119–20; and *Indianapolis News,* 7 June 1924.

22. Correspondence from Jacob Piatt Dunn to the *Indianapolis Saturday Herald,* 4 July 1879, scrapboook, Dunn Papers, IHS.

23. James A. Woodburn, *The Indiana Historical Society: A Hundred Years,* Indiana Historical Society *Publications,* vol. 10 (Indianapolis: The Bobbs-Merrill Co., 1933), 24.

24. Jacob Piatt Dunn, *The Omitted Paper: Municipal Financial Pressure, an Address before the Second Annual Conference on Taxation in Indiana, by J. P. Dunn, City Controller of Indianapolis* (Indianapolis: Premier Printing Co., 1914), 8.

25. Richard Hofstadter, *The Progressive Historians: Turner, Beard, Parrington* (New York: Alfred A. Knopf, 1968), 11.

26. For information on Dillon's life, see George S. Cottman, "John Brown Dillon: The Father of Indiana History," *Indiana Magazine of History* 1 (First Quarter 1905): 3–8, and Ray Boomhower, "The Father of

Indiana History and the Devil's Lake Monster," *Traces of Indiana and Midwestern History* 4 (winter 1992): 38–45.

27. Ruegamer, "History, Politics, and the Active Life," 265.

28. Ibid., 266–67.

29. Publishing agreement between Jacob Piatt Dunn and Harper & Brothers, 9 Nov. 1885, Dunn Papers, IHS.

30. Jacob Piatt Dunn, *Massacres of the Mountains: A History of the Indian Wars of the Far West, 1815–1875* (1886; reprint, New York: Archer House, 1958), 17, 32.

31. Ibid., 35.

32. Reviews of *Massacres of the Mountains, New York Examiner*, 29 Apr. 1886; *Denver Tribune-Republican*, 26 Apr. 1886; *Boston Globe*, 30 Apr. 1886; and *Indianapolis News*, 19 May 1886, scrapbook, Dunn Papers, IHS.

33. Theodore Roosevelt to Jacob Piatt Dunn, 22 Apr. 1888, ibid.

34. Dunn, *Indiana and Indianans*, 1:165–66. See also Ruegamer, "History, Politics, and the Active Life," 276–77.

35. Thornburg, *Earlham*, 156.

36. Jacob Piatt Dunn, *Indiana: A Redemption from Slavery* (1888; reprint, Cambridge, Mass.: Riverside Press, 1905), ix.

37. Ibid., 442.

38. *New York Times*, 14 Oct. 1888, and review of *Indiana: A Redemption from Slavery*, in *The Nation*, 24 Jan. 1889, scrapbook, Dunn Papers, IHS.

39. Dunn, *Indiana*, 109.

40. Contract between B. F. Bowen & Company and Jacob Piatt Dunn, Dunn Papers, IHS.

41. Dunn, *Greater Indianapolis*, 1:7–8.

42. Ibid., 1:241.

43. Ruegamer, "History, Politics, and the Active Life," 277.

44. Karl Detzer, *Myself When Young* (New York: Funk and Wagnalls, 1968), 9.

45. *Indianapolis Star*, 20 Aug. 1954.

46. Caroline Dunn, *Jacob Piatt Dunn*, 34–35.

47. "Jacob Dunn Was Man of Many Talents," *Reading in Indianapolis* (1 Jan. 1977) [a publication of the Indianapolis-Marion County Public Library]. See also Caroline Dunn, *Jacob Piatt Dunn*, 34–35.

48. Jacob Piatt Dunn to Caroline Dunn, 24 Aug. 1907, Caroline Dunn Papers, Indiana Historical Society Library, Indianapolis.

49. Jacob Piatt Dunn, "An Historical Detective Story," *Proceedings of the Mississippi Valley Historical Association . . . for the Year 1919–1920*, vol. 10, part 2 (Cedar Rapids, Iowa: Torch Press, 1921), 256–58. Dunn also urged young students of history not to abandon what he called "'knotty problems.'" Although there existed the possibility that one would never find the solution, Dunn believed that by making a practice

of saving puzzling questions for later study, "you are almost sure to find the solution of some of them; and if you do, you will have the material for a good historical story." Ibid., 258.

50. David Laurance Chambers to Samuel Duff McCoy, 25 Oct. 1955, Samuel Duff McCoy Papers, Lilly Library, Indiana University, Bloomington. In the letter, Chambers went on to complain that Dunn would often "gas at length at every meeting of the Literary Club but never by remotest chance on the subject of the paper. Generally he would get around to the Miami of Indiana; he knew a lot about the Injuns." Ibid.

51. See "Propylaeum Club to Fete Mrs. Dunn at Luncheon," *Indianapolis Star*, 13 January 1945, and "Mrs. Dunn, Widow of Historian Dies," *Indianapolis Star*, 12 April 1956.

52. Charlotte Dunn to Jacob Piatt Dunn, 4 Jan. 1922, box 1, folder 2, Dunn Papers, IHS.

53. Charlotte Dunn to Jacob Piatt Dunn, 20 Jan. 1922, ibid.

54. Jacob Piatt Dunn to Beloved Children, 11 Aug. 1920, Caroline Dunn Papers, IHS. See also "A Modern Martyr," undated speech, Dunn Papers, IHS, and Ruegamer, "History, Politics, and the Active Life," 281.

55. Dunn, "Historical Detective Story," 248.

Notes to Chapter 2

1. James A. Woodburn, *The Indiana Historical Society: A Hundred Years*, Indiana Historical Society *Publications,* vol. 10 (Indianapolis: The Bobbs-Merrill Co., 1933), 5–6. See also Lana Ruegamer, *A History of the Indiana Historical Society, 1830–1980* (Indianapolis: Indiana Historical Society, 1980), 9–26, and *Proceedings of the Indiana Historical Society, 1830–1886*, Indiana Historical Society *Publications*, vol. 1, no. 1 (Indianapolis: The Bowen-Merrill Co., 1897), 9–13.

2. *Proceedings of the Indiana Historical Society, 1830–1886*, p. 5.

3. Woodburn, *Indiana Historical Society*, 10.

4. *Proceedings of the Indiana Historical Society, 1830–1886*, p. 7. See also Ruegamer, *History of the Indiana Historical Society*, 78.

5. Ruegamer, *History of the Indiana Historical Society*, 85.

6. *Minutes of the Indiana Historical Society, 1886–1918*, Indiana Historical Society *Publications*, vol. 6, no. 4 (Indianapolis: C. E. Pauley and Co., 1919), 468.

7. Woodburn, *Indiana Historical Society*, 17.

8. *Minutes of the Society, 1886–1918*, p. 464.

9. Ruegamer, *History of the Indiana Historical Society*, 93. The agreement between the Indiana Historical Society and Bowen-Merrill changed at the turn of the century after the Society received a $600 appropriation from the Indiana legislature for publications in 1900 and 1901. The Society purchased the publishing firm's supply of Society's

publications, bought for $810, and Bowen-Merrill agreed to serve as the institution's agent for sales, thus ending its free printing of Society items. Ibid., 94.

10. Woodburn, *Indiana Historical Society*, 25.

11. *Proceedings of the Society, 1830–1886*, pp. 5–8. See also Ruegamer, *History of the Indiana Historical Society*, 84–85.

12. See Esther U. McNitt, "Short History of the Indiana State Library," *Library Occurrent* 10 (Jan.–Mar. 1931): 21–30; Larry Joe Barr, "The Indiana State Library, 1825–1925" (Ph.D. diss., Indiana University, 1976), 30–31; and Jacob Piatt Dunn, Jr., *Greater Indianapolis: The History, the Industries, the Institutions, and the People of a City of Homes*, 2 vols. (Chicago: The Lewis Publishing Co., 1910), 1:509.

13. McNitt, "Short History of the Indiana State Library," 22.

14. Lew Wallace, *Lew Wallace: An Autobiography* (1906; reprint, New York: Garrett Press, 1969), 54. See also Dunn, *Greater Indianapolis*, 1:509.

15. Ruegamer, *History of the Indiana Historical Society*, 94–95.

16. Dunn, *Greater Indianapolis*, 1:510. See also Ruegamer, *History of the Indiana Historical Society*, 95–96, and McNitt, "Short History of the Indiana State Library," 24–25.

17. Dunn, *Greater Indianapolis*, 1:510.

18. McNitt, "Short History of the Indiana State Library," 25. See also Ruegamer, *History of the Indiana Historical Society*, 96.

19. McNitt, "Short History of the Indiana State Library," 25.

20. Undated speech, Jacob Piatt Dunn, Jr., Papers, Indiana Division, Indiana State Library, Indianapolis.

21. Jacob Piatt Dunn, *Township Libraries for Indiana* (Richmond, Ind.: M. Cullaton and Co., 1890), 3–4. See also Jacob Piatt Dunn, *The Libraries of Indiana* (Indianapolis: Wm. B. Burford, 1893), 15–18.

22. Dunn, *Township Libraries for Indiana*, 5, and *Libraries of Indiana*, 18, 19.

23. Dunn, *Libraries of Indiana*, 31.

24. Jacob Piatt Dunn, *Indiana and Indianans: A History of Aboriginal and Territorial Indiana and the Century of Statehood*, 5 vols. (Chicago and New York: The American Historical Society, 1919), 2:920. See also William E. Henry, comp., *Municipal and Institutional Libraries of Indiana: History, Condition and Management* (Indianapolis: The Louisiana Purchase Exposition Commission of Indiana, 1904), 73–76; Clifton J. Phillips, *Indiana in Transition: The Emergence of an Industrial Commonwealth, 1880–1920* (Indianapolis: Indiana Historical Bureau and Indiana Historical Society, 1968), 402–3; and Hazel B. Warren, "The Indiana Public Library Commission," *Library Occurrent* 10 (Jan.–Mar. 1931): 31–35.

25. See Henry, comp., *Municipal and Institutional Libraries of Indiana*, 73, and Warren, "Indiana Public Library Commission," 31.

26. Dunn, *Indiana and Indianans*, 2:921, and Henry, comp., *Municipal and Institutional Libraries of Indiana*, 74, 75.

27. Jacob Piatt Dunn, *Township Libraries: Aids to Indiana Schools* (Indianapolis: Journal Job Printing Co., 1892), 11.

Notes to Chapter 3

1. *New York Times*, 24 Nov. 1889.

2. Lana Ruegamer, *A History of the Indiana Historical Society, 1830–1980* (Indianapolis: Indiana Historical Society, 1980), 83–86, and "History, Politics, and the Active Life: Jacob Piatt Dunn, Progressive Historian," *Indiana Magazine of History* 81 (Sept. 1985): 272.

3. *The Tobacco Trust and Local Interests: Speech of J. P. Dunn, Democratic Candidate for Congress, at John Rauch's Cigar Factory, October 21, 1902* (Indianapolis: Allied Printing, [1902]). For more on Dunn's nomination, see *Indianapolis Sentinel*, 7 Sept. 1902, and *Indianapolis Journal*, 7 Sept. 1902.

4. Philip R. VanderMeer, *The Hoosier Politician: Officeholding and Political Culture in Indiana, 1896–1920* (Urbana: University of Illinois Press, 1985), 25.

5. Louis Ludlow, *From Cornfield to Press Gallery: Adventures and Reminiscences of a Veteran Washington Correspondent* (Washington, D.C.: W. F. Roberts Co., 1924), 96.

6. Claude Bowers, *My Life: The Memoirs of Claude Bowers* (New York: Simon and Schuster, 1962), 40.

7. *Indianapolis Sentinel*, 24 May 1894.

8. Quoted in Charlotte Ethel Bruce, "A Review of Indiana Election Laws, 1889–1935" (M.A. thesis, Butler University, 1935), 1.

9. Anna Marie Sander, "A Review of the Election Laws in the State of Indiana from 1787 to 1890" (M.A. thesis, Butler University, 1933), 31. For a discussion of the party ticket ballot, see George C. Roberts, "Indiana's Australian Ballot: Reform Tempered by the Political Environment," *Proceedings of the Indiana Academy of the Social Sciences*, 3d ser., 29 (21 Oct. 1994): 149.

10. Matthew Josephson, *The Politicos, 1865–1896* (New York: Harcourt, Brace and Co., 1938), 432.

11. Eldon Cobb Evans, *A History of the Australian Ballot System in the United States* (Chicago: The University of Chicago Press, 1917), 11. Nineteenth-century elections were often a popular spectator sport with wide community involvement. Speeches and rallies drew thousands of spectators, and the parties produced reams of literature touting their candidates. Jonathan P. Dolliver of Iowa spoke for many when he noted: "The man who, having the right to vote, is too lazy or too high-toned to mingle with his fellow citizens at the polls is the merest ape and echo of a citizen." See Lewis L. Gould, *Reform and*

Regulation: American Politics, 1900–1916 (New York: John Wiley and Sons, 1978), 4.

12. Josephson, *Politicos*, 430.

13. "Correspondence," *The Nation*, 22 Nov. 1888, p. 412.

14. Thomas Riley Marshall, *Recollections of Thomas R. Marshall, Vice-President and Hoosier Philosopher: A Hoosier Salad* (Indianapolis: Bobbs-Merrill Co., 1925), 139, 140.

15. *Indianapolis Journal*, 2 Nov. 1888.

16. Charles W. Calhoun, *Gilded Age Cato: The Life of Walter Q. Gresham* (Lexington, Ky.: The University Press of Kentucky, 1988), 103–4.

17. *Indianapolis Sentinel*, 31 Oct. 1888. See also Roger A. Fischer, "'Blocks of Five' Dudley, Cartoon Celebrity," *Indiana Magazine of History* 87 (Dec. 1991): 334–47, and Jacob Piatt Dunn, Jr., *Greater Indianapolis: The History, the Industries, the Institutions, and the People of a City of Homes*, 2 vols. (Chicago: The Lewis Publishing Co., 1910), 1:298.

18. Bruce, "Review of Indiana Election Laws," 3–4.

19. Dunn, *Greater Indianapolis*, 1:300.

20. The role vote fraud played in electing Harrison, and ballot box corruption in general during the Gilded Age, has been a subject of much scholarly debate. Corruption, according to Eugene Roseboom, was the "deciding factor" in Harrison's Indiana win. In his biography of Grover Cleveland, Allan Nevins blames the incumbent's defeat on the bribing of voters in Indiana and New York. H. Wayne Morgan, however, claimed that both Democrats and Republicans used bribes to sway voters in the election and "probably canceled each other's efforts." For further discussion on vote buying's role in the 1888 election, see R. C. Buley, "The Campaign of 1888 in Indiana," *Indiana Magazine of History* 10 (June 1914): 30–53; Richard Jensen, *The Winning of the Midwest: Social and Political Conflict, 1888–1896* (Chicago: The University of Chicago Press, 1971), 27–29; H. Wayne Morgan, *From Hayes to McKinley: National Party Politics, 1877–1896* (Syracuse, N.Y.: Syracuse University Press, 1969), 310–12; John E. McDaniel, Jr., "The Presidential Election of 1888" (Ph.D. diss., The University of Texas at Austin, 1970), 195; Allan Nevins, *Grover Cleveland: A Study in Courage* (New York: Dodd, Mead and Co., 1933), 436–37; and Eugene H. Roseboom, *A History of Presidential Elections* (New York: Macmillan, 1957), 282–83. For a comprehensive review of election fraud during this era, see Peter H. Argersinger, "New Perspectives on Election Fraud in the Gilded Age," *Political Science Quarterly* 100 (winter 1985–86): 669–87.

21. James A. Kehl, *Boss Rule in the Gilded Age: Matt Quay of Pennsylvania* (Pittsburgh: University of Pittsburgh Press, 1981), 116–17. Harrison and other nineteenth-century politicians had what Robert H. Wiebe has called a "segmented morality," with different parts of their

lives occupying different positions and each judged accordingly. This enabled knowledgeable politicians like Harrison, said Wiebe, to disregard the "unsavory tactics" that won him the presidency and still be able to walk "in the light as God's humble servants." See Robert H. Wiebe, *The Search for Order, 1877–1920* (New York: Hill and Wang, 1967), 40.

22. Dunn, *Greater Indianapolis*, 1:306.

23. Evans, *History of the Australian Ballot System*, 21. See also L. E. Fredman, *The Australian Ballot: The Story of an American Reform* (East Lansing: Michigan State University Press, 1968). For Indiana's experience with the Australian system, see Robert LaFollette, "The Adoption of the Australian Ballot in Indiana," *Indiana Magazine of History* 24 (June 1928): 105–20.

24. *Indianapolis Sentinel*, 19 Nov. 1888.

25. Jacob Piatt Dunn, *Indiana and Indianans: A History of Aboriginal and Territorial Indiana and the Century of Statehood*, 5 vols. (Chicago and New York: The American Historical Society, 1919), 2:744–46.

26. Indiana *House Journal* (1889), 63, 65.

27. *Indianapolis Sentinel*, 17 Jan. 1889.

28. Dunn, *Indiana and Indianans*, 2:745. According to David Sarasohn, Democratic reform efforts in the late nineteenth and early twentieth centuries often were marked by a "healthy dose of self-interest," particularly when it involved the party's "unvarying scarcity of funds" as compared with the GOP (i.e., Democrat support for full disclosure of campaign contributions). See David Sarasohn, *The Party of Reform: Democrats in the Progressive Era* (Jackson: University Press of Mississippi, 1989), xi–xii.

29. Dunn, *Greater Indianapolis*, 1:307.

30. *Indianapolis News*, 21 Dec. 1908.

31. Clifton J. Phillips, *Indiana in Transition: The Emergence of an Industrial Commonwealth, 1880–1920* (Indianapolis: Indiana Historical Bureau and Indiana Historical Society, 1968), 30. See also Justin E. Walsh, *The Centennial History of the Indiana General Assembly, 1816–1978* (Indianapolis: The Select Committee on the Centennial History of the Indiana General Assembly, in cooperation with the Indiana Historical Bureau, 1987), 228–29, and Roberts, "Indiana's Australian Ballot," 154.

32. George C. Roberts, "The Vanishing Indiana Ballot," *Proceedings of the Indiana Academy of the Social Sciences,* 3d ser., 26 (11 Oct. 1991): 139–40.

33. Dunn, *Greater Indianapolis*, 1:306.

34. *Indianapolis News*, 2 Jan. 1890.

35. Jerrold G. Rusk, "The Effect of the Australian Ballot Reform on Split Ticket Voting: 1876–1908," *American Political Science Review* 64 (Dec. 1970): 1221.

36. *Indianapolis Sentinel*, 12 Feb., 7 Mar. 1889.
37. Dunn, *Greater Indianapolis*, 1:307–8.
38. Dunn, *Indiana and Indianans*, 2:769.

Notes to Chapter 4

1. William A. Blomquist, "Government," in David J. Bodenhamer and Robert G. Barrows, eds., *The Encyclopedia of Indianapolis* (Bloomington and Indianapolis: Indiana University Press, 1994), 89.

2. Hester Anne Hale, *Indianapolis: The First Century* (Indianapolis: Marion County/Indianapolis Historical Society, 1987), 42–43, 44, 51.

3. Jacob Piatt Dunn, Jr., *Greater Indianapolis: The History, the Industries, the Institutions, and the People of a City of Homes*, 2 vols. (Chicago: The Lewis Publishing Co., 1910), 1:309–10.

4. Ibid., 1:309–10, 311. See also John Bartlow Martin, *Indiana: An Interpretation* (1947; reprint, Bloomington and Indianapolis: Indiana University Press, 1992), 93.

5. Dunn, *Greater Indianapolis*, 1:309–10. See also Charles Latham, Jr., *William Fortune (1863–1942): A Hoosier Biography* (Indianapolis: Guild Press of Indiana, 1994), 47.

6. Dunn, *Greater Indianapolis*, 1:310–11.

7. *Indianapolis News*, 10 Feb. 1890, and "Street Paving Exposition," in Bodenhamer and Barrows, eds., *Encyclopedia of Indianapolis*, 1302.

8. Samuel P. Hays, *The Response to Industrialism, 1885–1914* (Chicago and London: The University of Chicago Press, 1957), 104, 107. Hays also contends that the movement for reform of municipal government came not from the lower or middle classes, but from the upper class, especially the leading business groups. Such organizations allied themselves with professional men and "initiated and dominated municipal movements," a theory that fits well with the genesis of Indianapolis's new city charter. See Hays, "The Politics of Reform in Municipal Government in the Progressive Era," *Pacific Northwest Quarterly* 55 (Oct. 1964): 159.

9. Martin J. Schiesl, *The Politics of Efficiency: Municipal Administration and Reform in America, 1880–1920* (Berkeley: University of California Press, 1977), 3. See also Ernest S. Griffith, *A History of American City Government: The Conspicuous Failure, 1870–1900* (New York: Praeger Publishers, 1974), 107–8. Griffith had great respect for Indianapolis's 1891 charter, calling it, for its time, "one of the very best by reformist standards." Ibid., 246.

10. Dunn, *Greater Indianapolis*, 1:312, 313.

11. Ibid., 1:313.

12. Ibid., 1:313, 314, 320.

13. *Indianapolis Journal*, 23 Jan. 1891. See also Dunn, *Greater Indianapolis*, 1:317.

14. Dunn, *Greater Indianapolis,* 1:317.
15. Ibid., 1:317–18.
16. *Indianapolis Sentinel,* 27 Jan. 1891.
17. Dunn, *Greater Indianapolis,* 1:318. See also *Indianapolis Sentinel,* 28 Jan. 1891.
18. Dunn, *Greater Indianapolis,* 1:318–20.
19. *Indianapolis Sentinel,* 1 Mar. 1891.
20. Ibid., 2 Mar. 1891.
21. Ibid., 3 Mar. 1891.
22. Indiana *Senate Journal* (1891), 968.
23. *Indianapolis Sentinel,* 4 Mar. 1891.
24. *Indianapolis News,* 13 Jan. 1916.
25. Ibid., 13 July 1916, and *Indianapolis Star,* 13 July 1916.
26. *Indianapolis News,* 13 July 1916.
27. *Indianapolis Star,* 13, 14 July 1916.
28. *Indianapolis News,* 13 July 1916.

Notes to Chapter 5

1. Ralph D. Gray, *Indiana's Favorite Sons, 1840–1940* (Indianapolis: Indiana Historical Society, 1988), 27.
2. Indiana *Senate Journal* (1911), 23.
3. Ibid., 24.
4. Indiana *House Journal* (1911), 1758.
5. Charles M. Thomas, *Thomas Riley Marshall: Hoosier Statesman* (Oxford, Ohio: Mississippi Valley Press, 1939), 88.
6. Thomas Riley Marshall, *Recollections of Thomas Riley Marshall, Vice-President and Hoosier Philosopher: A Hoosier Salad* (Indianapolis: Bobbs-Merrill Co., 1925), 151.
7. Louis Ludlow, *From Cornfield to Press Gallery: Adventures and Reminiscences of a Veteran Washington Correspondent* (Washington, D.C.: W. F. Roberts Co., 1924), 396.
8. Marshall, *Recollections,* 159–61.
9. Ibid., 166–67, 169–70.
10. Keith S. Montgomery, "Thomas R. Marshall's Victory in the Election of 1908," *Indiana Magazine of History* 53 (June 1957): 159.
11. James E. Watson, *As I Knew Them: Memoirs of James E. Watson* (Indianapolis and New York: Bobbs-Merrill Co., 1936), 208. Watson recalled that the experience of his mother's first cousin, Gen. Thomas M. Browne, GOP nominee for Indiana governor in 1872 who was beaten by Democrat Thomas Hendricks, paralleled his own: "General Browne was defeated by Governor Hendricks on the temperance question, and Tom Marshall beat me on the same issue. In remarking to Marshall on the matter one day, I said to him that I thought the temperance issue was a mighty bad one for my family. Whereupon Marshall remarked: 'No,

Jim, your family is a damned bad family for the temperance issue.'"
Ibid., 19.

12. Indiana *Senate Journal* (1909), 107–8.

13. Jacob Piatt Dunn, *Indiana and Indianans: A History of Aboriginal and Territorial Indiana and the Century of Statehood*, 5 vols. (Chicago and New York: The American Historical Society, 1919), 2:748.

14. Richard John Del Vecchio, "Indiana Politics during the Progressive Era, 1912–1916" (Ph.D. diss., University of Notre Dame, 1973), 39. According to Del Vecchio, reform was an integral part of the Hoosier State "long before the fulminations of [Theodore] Roosevelt, the exposes of the muckrakers, or the revolt of the Republican insurgents." Ibid., v.

15. Marshall address to Democratic State Convention, 27 Apr. 1910, Thomas R. Marshall Papers, Indiana Division, Indiana State Library, Indianapolis.

16. Marshall, *Recollections*, 178.

17. Charles Kettleborough, *Constitution Making in Indiana: A Source Book of Constitutional Documents with Historical Introduction and Critical Notes*, 3 vols. (Indianapolis: Indiana Historical Commission, 1916, 1930), 2:338–39. See also John D. Barnhart and Donald F. Carmony, *Indiana's Century Old Constitution* (Indianapolis: State Constitution Centennial Commission, 1951), 17–18, 51.

18. *Indianapolis News*, 21 Dec. 1908.

19. Ibid., 13 Feb. 1911.

20. Robert Luce, *Legislative Principles: The History and Theory of Lawmaking by Representative Government* (Boston and New York: Houghton Mifflin Co., 1930), 140.

21. *Indianapolis News*, 14 Feb. 1911.

22. Dunn, *Indiana and Indianans*, 2:771, 772.

23. Jacob Piatt Dunn, "Duty of the State to Its History," *Indiana Magazine of History* 6 (Dec. 1910): 142–43.

24. Caroline Dunn, telephone conversation with author, 7 Feb. 1992.

25. *Indianapolis City Directory, 1911* (Indianapolis: R. L. Polk and Co., 1911), 507, 1026.

26. Jacob Piatt Dunn, *The Proposed Constitution of Indiana* (Indianapolis: Sentinel Printing Co., 1911), 4.

27. Ibid., 9. The 1816 Constitution states in Article VIII, Section 1, that: "Every twelfth year, after this constitution shall have taken effect, at the general election held for Governor there shall be a poll opened, in which the qualified Electors of the State shall express by vote, whether they are in favour of calling a convention, or not, and if there should be a majority of all the votes given at such election . . . the Governor shall inform the next General Assembly thereof, whose duty it shall be to provide, by law, for the election of the members to the convention." See Kettleborough, *Constitution Making in Indiana*, 1:111–12.

28. John D. Barnhart and Donald F. Carmony, *Indiana: From Frontier to Industrial Commonwealth*, 4 vols. (New York: Lewis Historical Publishing Co., 1954), 2:83–85.

29. Dunn, *Proposed Constitution of Indiana*, 11.

30. Ibid., 22.

31. Ibid., addendum, 1–8. See also Clifton J. Phillips, *Indiana in Transition: The Emergence of an Industrial Commonwealth, 1880–1920* (Indianapolis: Indiana Historical Bureau and Indiana Historical Society, 1968), 111.

32. Thomas R. Marshall to Theodore W. Noyes, Washington D.C., 17 May 1913, Marshall Papers, Indiana State Library.

33. Jacob P. Dunn, "The Proposed Constitution of Indiana," *Indiana Magazine of History* 7 (Sept. 1911): 100.

34. Dunn, *Proposed Constitution of Indiana*, 26.

35. Richard Hofstadter, *The Age of Reform: From Bryan to F.D.R.* (New York: Vantage Books, 1955), 178.

36. Dunn, *Proposed Constitution of Indiana*, addendum, 1, 2.

37. A. James Reichley, *The Life of the Parties: A History of American Political Parties* (New York: The Free Press, 1992), 208–9.

38. See Roger Daniels, *Coming to America: A History of Immigration and Ethnicity in American Life* (New York: HarperCollins, 1990), 278; John Higham, *Strangers in the Land: Patterns of American Nativism, 1860–1925* (New Brunswick, N.J.: Rutgers University Press, 1955), 203; and Robert H. Wiebe, *The Search for Order, 1877–1920* (New York: Hill and Wang, 1967), 210.

39. Undated speech [given to the American Political Science Association annual meeting, 27–30 December 1911], p. 9, Jacob Piatt Dunn Papers, Indiana Historical Society Library, Indianapolis (hereafter cited as Dunn Papers, IHS). Text reprinted as "The Proposed Legislative Constitution of Indiana," *Proceedings of the American Political Science Association,* in *American Political Science Review* 6 (1912): 43–52, Supplement.

40. In the late 1840s and early 1850s, many states in the West believed that any "arduous restrictions on the vote or any other fundamental rights would discourage newcomers." See William J. Crotty, *Political Reform and the American Experiment* (New York: Thomas Y. Crowell Co., 1977), 19–20.

41. Undated speech, p. 9, Dunn Papers, IHS.

42. Ibid., 12–13.

43. Thomas R. Marshall to Henry Barnhart, 17 Feb. 1911, Letter Book 56 (11 July 1910–23 Mar. 1912), Thomas R. Marshall Papers, Indiana State Archives, Commission on Public Records, Indianapolis.

44. *Indianapolis News*, 2 June 1911.

45. *Indianapolis Star*, 15 Feb. 1911.

46. Ibid., 17 Feb. 1911.

47. Ibid., 17, 18 Feb. 1911.

48. Ibid., 16 Feb. 1911.

49. Ibid., 18 Feb. 1911.

50. Dunn, *Proposed Constitution of Indiana*, 47.

51. *Indianapolis Star*, 14 Feb. 1911.

52. Marshall to Barnhart, 17 Feb. 1911, Letter Book 56, Marshall Papers, Indiana State Archives.

53. Marshall to Barnhart, 22 Feb. 1911, ibid.

54. *Indianapolis News*, 2 June 1911.

55. James A. Woodburn to Grace Julian Clarke, 22 Mar. 1911, Grace Julian Clarke Papers, Indiana Division, Indiana State Library, Indianapolis.

56. James A. Woodburn, *Why Indiana Needs a New Constitution* (Indianapolis: Woman's Franchise League of Indiana, 1913), 6.

57. Dunn, *Indiana and Indianans*, 2:771, 776.

58. *Indianapolis Star*, 18 Feb. 1911.

59. Dunn, *Indiana and Indianans*, 2:771.

60. Undated speech, p. 5, Dunn Papers, IHS.

61. *Ellingham* v. *Dye*, 178 Ind. 336, 341 (1912).

62. Ibid., 381.

63. Ibid., 439.

64. Marshall, *Recollections*, 210, 214.

65. Ibid., 213.

66. Ibid., 214.

67. *Indianapolis Star*, 2 Dec. 1913.

68. Dunn, *Indiana and Indianans*, 2:775–76.

69. Ibid., 2:776.

70. Jacob Piatt Dunn, *The Constitutional Amendments and the Democratic Party: An Address Delivered June 17th, 1921 to the Indiana Democratic Club of Indianapolis* (Greenfield, Ind.: Wm. Mitchell Printing Co., 1921), 16.

71. Ibid., 4.

72. Jacob Piatt Dunn, *The Negro Issue: An Address by Jacob Piatt Dunn, City Controller of Indianapolis, before the Indiana Democratic Club, October 13, 1904* (Indianapolis: Sentinel Printing Co., 1904), 17, 22. See also *Indianapolis News*, 14 Oct. 1904.

73. Emma Lou Thornbrough, *The Negro in Indiana before 1900: A Study of a Minority* (1957; reprint, Bloomington: Indiana University Press, 1993), 239. Blacks in Indiana did not forget the Democratic party's efforts against them. When the Fifteenth Amendment was ratified, Rev. Moses Broyles, at a celebration in Indianapolis, advised his fellow African Americans "above all to stick to the party of freedom, the party of liberty. Vote a straight Republican ticket at the next election, without any scratching." It was a call to arms that blacks followed for years to come. Ibid., 252. See also James H. Madison, *The Indiana Way: A State History* (Bloomington and Indiana-

polis: Indiana University Press and Indiana Historical Society, 1986), 169–71.

74. Charles Kettleborough, *Constitution Making in Indiana*, 3:193–94, 221–30.

75. Ibid., 3:231.

76. John A. Bremer, *Constitution Making in Indiana: A Source Book of Constitutional Documents, with Historical Introduction and Critical Notes* (Indianapolis: Indiana Historical Bureau, 1978), vii–viii.

77. Luce, *Legislative Principles*, 140.

78. Albert Lee Sturm, *Methods of State Constitutional Reform* (Ann Arbor: University of Michigan Press, 1954), 23.

79. Justin E. Walsh, *The Centennial History of the Indiana General Assembly, 1816–1978* (Indianapolis: The Select Committee on the Centennial History of the Indiana General Assembly, in cooperation with the Indiana Historical Bureau, 1987), 329, 335. See also *Indianapolis Star*, 19 Jan. 1925.

80. For the national figures see Frances Fox Piven and Richard A. Cloward, *Why Americans Don't Vote* (New York: Pantheon Books, 1989), 54–55; for Indiana's totals see Del Vecchio, "Indiana Politics during the Progressive Era," 35–36.

Notes to Chapter 6

1. Jacob Piatt Dunn, *True Indian Stories* (Indianapolis: Sentinel Printing Co., 1909), 10.

2. Jacob Piatt Dunn, "Misunderstood Mythology," *Americana* (Apr. 1923): 180.

3. Stewart Rafert, *The Miami Indians of Indiana: A Persistent People, 1654–1994* (Indianapolis: Indiana Historical Society, 1996), 192.

4. Dunn, "Misunderstood Mythology," 183.

5. Caroline Dunn, *Jacob Piatt Dunn: His Miami Language Studies and Indian Manuscript Collection, Prehistory Research Series*, vol. 1, no. 2 (Indianapolis: Indiana Historical Society, 1937), 35.

6. Jacob Piatt Dunn, *Indiana: A Redemption from Slavery* (1888; reprint, Cambridge, Mass.: The Riverside Press, 1905), 15 n. 3. See also Lana Ruegamer, "History, Politics, and the Active Life: Jacob Piatt Dunn, Progressive Historian," *Indiana Magazine of History* 81 (Sept. 1985): 277.

7. James Mooney to Jacob Piatt Dunn, 17 Nov. 1888, Indian Materials, Correspondence, #45, Jacob Piatt Dunn, Jr., Papers, Indiana Division, Indiana State Library, Indianapolis (hereafter cited as Dunn Papers, ISL).

8. Review of *True Indian Stories* in January–March 1908 issue of *American Anthropologist*, ibid.

9. Dunn, *True Indian Stories*, 10–11.

10. Jacob Piatt Dunn, *Indiana and Indianans: A History of Aboriginal and Territorial Indiana and the Century of Statehood,* 5 vols. (Chicago and New York: The American Historical Society, 1919), 1:43–44. See also Rafert, *Miami Indians of Indiana*, 198.

11. *Indianapolis Journal*, 7 Jan. 1900.

12. Dunn, *Indiana and Indianans*, 1:44.

13. Caroline Dunn, *Jacob Piatt Dunn*, 37–38.

14. Jacob Piatt Dunn to W. H. Holmes, 18 May 1909, Indian Materials, Correspondence, #46, Dunn Papers, ISL. See also Caroline Dunn, *Jacob Piatt Dunn*, 38–39.

15. Caroline Dunn, *Jacob Piatt Dunn,* 39.

16. Dunn to Holmes, 18 May 1909, Indian Materials, Correspondence, #46, Dunn Papers, ISL.

17. Undated letter, Indian Materials, Correspondence, #62, ibid.

18. Caroline Dunn, *Jacob Piatt Dunn,* 40.

19. C. F. Voegelin, *Shawnee Stems and the Jacob P. Dunn Miami Dictionary, Part I, Stems in p-, Prehistory Research Series,* vol. 1, no. 3 (Indianapolis: Indiana Historical Society, 1938), 63. See also Ruegamer, "History, Politics, and the Active Life," 279.

20. Caroline Dunn, *Jacob Piatt Dunn*, 42.

21. Jacob Piatt Dunn, "Misunderstood Mythology," 184.

22. Ibid.

23. *Indianapolis Star*, 7 Apr. 1907.

24. *Indianapolis News*, 25 Apr. 1907.

25. *Indianapolis Star*, 28 Apr. 1907.

26. "Editorial and Miscellaneous," *Indiana Magazine of History* 3 (June 1907): 96.

27. *Proceedings of Second Annual State History Conference, under Auspices of the Society of Indiana Pioneers, Indianapolis, December 10–11, 1920* (Fort Wayne: Fort Wayne Printing Co., 1921), 21–24. See also Ruegamer, "History, Politics, and the Active Life," 279.

28. Caroline Dunn, *Jacob Piatt Dunn*, 42.

29. Rafert, *Miami Indians of Indiana*, 194.

30. *Federal Register,* vol. 60, no. 173 (7 Sept. 1995).

Notes to Conclusion

1. *Indianapolis Star*, 25 June 1913.

2. Ibid., 27 Jan. 1922.

3. Caroline Dunn to Professor Grant, undated letter, Caroline Dunn Papers, Indiana Historical Society Library, Indianapolis.

4. Richard Lieber to Hon. Medill McCormick, 15 Dec. 1921, Jacob Piatt Dunn Papers, Indiana Historical Society Library, Indianapolis (hereafter cited as Dunn Papers, IHS).

Notes

5. Log of a San Domingonaut, box 2, folder 6, ibid.

6. Ibid.

7. Ibid.

8. Jacob Piatt Dunn to Eleanor Dunn, 22 Jan. 1922, box 1, folder 2, Dunn Papers, IHS.

9. Log of a San Domingonaut, ibid.

10. Rayford W. Logan, *Haiti and the Dominican Republic* (New York and London: Oxford University Press, 1968), 6.

11. Log of a San Domingonaut, Dunn Papers, IHS.

12. Charlotte Dunn to Jacob Piatt Dunn, 20 Jan. 1922, and late Jan. or early Feb. 1922, ibid.

13. Log of a San Domingonaut, ibid.

14. Ibid.; *Indianapolis News*, 6 May 1922.

15. Log of a San Domingonaut, and Jacob Piatt Dunn to Charlotte Dunn, 22 Jan. 1922, Dunn Papers, IHS.

16. Log of a San Domingonaut, ibid.

17. Ibid.

18. Charlotte Dunn to Jacob Piatt Dunn, late Jan. or early Feb. 1922, Dunn Papers, IHS.

19. Log of a San Domingonaut, ibid.

20. *Indianapolis Star*, 27 Jan. 1922; and Lana Ruegamer, "History, Politics, and the Active Life: Jacob Piatt Dunn, Progressive Historian," *Indiana Magazine of History* 81 (Sept. 1985): 281.

21. *Indianapolis News*, 10 Apr. 1922.

22. Ibid., 15 Apr. 1922.

23. Ibid., 22 Apr. 1922.

24. Jacob Piatt Dunn to Samuel M. Ralston, 27 Mar. 1922, Samuel M. Ralston Papers, Lilly Library, Indiana University, Bloomington.

25. Jacob Piatt Dunn to Caroline Dunn, 5 Jan. 1924, Caroline Dunn Papers, IHS.

26. Jacob Piatt Dunn, to Caroline Dunn, 6 Jan. 1924, ibid.

27. *Indianapolis News,* 7 June 1924.

28. Ibid.

29. Ruegamer, "History, Politics, and the Active Life," 282.

30. William Manchester, *The Last Lion, Winston Spencer Churchill: Visions of Glory, 1874–1932* (New York: Dell Publishing, 1983), 25–26.

31. Jacob Piatt Dunn, "Duty of the State to Its History," *Indiana Magazine of History* 6 (Dec. 1910): 143.

Bibliographical Essay

LISTED BELOW ARE THE WORKS THAT WERE OF THE GREATEST HELP IN PREPARing this work. By no means a complete record, this essay does substantially cover those primary and secondary sources that would be most useful to those wishing to explore the life of Jacob Piatt Dunn, Jr., and Indiana history and politics during the late nineteenth and early twentieth centuries.

Jacob Piatt Dunn, Jr.

In examining the life and times of Jacob Piatt Dunn, Jr., the greatest resource available has been the work of Dunn himself. Never shy about expounding on his role in the political maneuverings of his time, Dunn deals with the reform efforts he championed in both *Greater Indianapolis: The History, the Industries, the Institutions, and the People of a City of Homes*, 2 vols. (Chicago: The Lewis Publishing Co., 1910) and *Indiana and Indianans: A History of Aboriginal and Territorial Indiana and the Century of Statehood*, 5 vols. (Chicago and New York: The American Historical Society, 1919). The Hoosier historian's papers located in the Indiana State Library and the Indiana Historical Society Library also provide valuable insights into Dunn the reformer.

Dunn, a prolific writer, offered glimpses into his beliefs through a variety of works for numerous publications. Those that proved to be most helpful for this work included "Duty of the State to Its History," *Indiana Magazine of History* 6 (December 1910): 137–43; "Shall Indian Languages Be Preserved?" *Journal of the Illinois State Historical Society* 10 (April 1917): 87–96; *The New Tax Law of Indiana and the Science of Taxation* (Indianapolis: Sentinel Printing Co., 1892); *The Omitted Paper: Municipal Financial Pressure, an Address before the Second Annual Conference on Taxation in Indiana by J. P. Dunn, City Controller of Indianapolis* (Indianapolis: Premier Printing Co., 1914); *The Real Trouble with the Indiana Tax Law: An Address by J. P. Dunn, City Controller of Indianapolis, at the Bloomington Tax Conference, February 5 and 6,*

1914 (n.p., 1914); *Why is a Democrat? Speech of Hon. Jacob P. Dunn on the Issues of the Present City Campaign, before the Democratic Business Men's Meeting at the Denison Hotel, September 26, 1913* (Indianapolis: n.p., n.d.); *The Negro Issue: An Address by Jacob Piatt Dunn, City Controller of Indianapolis, before the Indiana Democratic Club, October 13, 1904* (Indianapolis: Sentinel Printing Co., 1904); *The Unknown God and Other Orthodox Essays* (Indianapolis: Sentinel Printing Co., 1914); and "An Historical Detective Story," *Proceedings of the Mississippi Valley Historical Association . . . for the Year 1919–1920,* 10, Pt. 2 (Cedar Rapids, Iowa: Torch Press, 1921).

There are only a few scholarly works on Dunn and his life, but those were extremely helpful for this effort. Particularly valuable was Lana Ruegamer's "History, Politics, and the Active Life: Jacob Piatt Dunn, Progressive Historian," *Indiana Magazine of History* 81 (September 1985): 265–83, and her examination of Dunn's relationship with the Indiana Historical Society in her book *A History of the Indiana Historical Society, 1830–1980* (Indianapolis: Indiana Historical Society, 1980). Other works detailing Dunn and the Indiana Historical Society include James A. Woodburn's *The Indiana Historical Society: A Hundred Years,* Indiana Historical Society *Publications,* vol. 10 (Indianapolis: The Bobbs-Merrill Co., 1933) and *Proceedings of the Indiana Historical Society, 1830–1886,* Indiana Historical Society *Publications,* vol. 1, no. 1 (Indianapolis: The Bowen-Merrill Co., 1897). Another study that provided essential information on Dunn's life was Caroline Dunn's *Jacob Piatt Dunn: His Miami Language Studies and Indian Manuscript Collection, Prehistory Research Series,* vol. 1, no. 2 (Indianapolis: Indiana Historical Society, 1937).

Contemporaries of Dunn offered their assessments of the Democratic reformer and historian, and the experience of working for partisan newspapers like the *Indianapolis Sentinel,* in such works as Claude Bowers's *My Life: The Memoirs of Claude Bowers* (New York: Simon and Schuster, 1962); Karl Detzer, *Myself When Young* (New York: Funk and Wagnalls, 1968); and Louis Ludlow, *From Cornfield to Press Gallery: Adventures and Reminiscences of a Veteran Washington Correspondent* (Washington, D.C.: W. F. Roberts Co., 1924).

For Dunn's place in the Progressive Era, and the reasons for his crusading spirit, Robert Morse Crunden's *Ministers of Reform: The Progressives' Achievement in American Civilization, 1889–1920* (New York: Basic Books, 1982), especially the role of parents on the subsequent careers of progressives like Dunn, was invaluable to this work. The following works also offered background on the Progressive Era and reform in the late nineteenth and early twentieth centuries: Richard Hofstadter, *The Age of Reform: From Bryan to F.D.R.* (New York: Vintage Books, 1955), and *The Progressive Historians: Turner, Beard, Parrington* (New York: Alfred A. Knopf, 1968); Keith W. Olson, *Biography of a Progressive:*

Franklin K. Lane, 1864–1921 (Westport, Conn.: Greenwood Press, 1979); Arthur S. Link and Richard L. McCormick, *Progressivism* (Arlington Heights, Ill.: Harlan Davidson, 1983); Daniel T. Rodgers, "In Search of Progressivism," *Reviews in American History* 10 (1982): 113–32; William J. Crotty, *Political Reform and the American Experiment* (New York: Thomas Y. Crowell Co., 1977); John D. Buenker, *Urban Liberalism and Progressive Reform* (New York: Scribner, 1973); and Russel B. Nye, *Midwestern Progressive Politics: A Historical Study of Its Origins and Development, 1870–1958* (East Lansing: Michigan State University Press, 1959).

For Dunn's time as state librarian and for a history of the Indiana State Library, see Esther U. McNitt's "Short History of the Indiana State Library," *Library Occurrent* (January-March 1931): 21–30; Larry Joe Barr's "The Indiana State Library, 1825–1925" (Ph.D. diss., Indiana University, 1976); and William E. Henry, comp., *Municipal and Institutional Libraries of Indiana: History, Condition and Management* (Indianapolis: The Louisiana Purchase Exposition Commission of Indiana, 1904). Dunn discusses the importance of free public libraries in such works as *Township Libraries for Indiana* (Richmond, Ind.: M. Cullaton Co., 1890), *Township Libraries: Aids to Indiana Schools* (Indianapolis: Journal Job Printing Co., 1892), and *The Libraries of Indiana* (Indianapolis: Wm. Burford, 1893).

Indiana Politics and the Australian Ballot Issue

The Hoosier State's prominence in national politics at the turn of the century drove many of Dunn's attempts at reform. The most comprehensive examination of this time period can be found in Clifton J. Phillips's *Indiana in Transition: The Emergence of an Industrial Commonwealth, 1880–1920* (Indianapolis: Indiana Historical Bureau and Indiana Historical Society, 1968). For a shorter synopsis of the nineteenth state's political past, see Ralph D. Gray's *Indiana's Favorite Sons, 1840–1940* (Indianapolis: Indiana Historical Society, 1988). The importance of Indiana in politics, and the high level of partisanship that existed in the state during the late nineteenth and early twentieth centuries, are also covered in Melvyn Hammarberg's *The Indiana Voter: The Historical Dynamics of Party Allegiance during the 1870s* (Chicago: The University of Chicago Press, 1977), and Philip R. VanderMeer's *The Hoosier Politician: Officeholding and Political Culture in Indiana, 1896–1920* (Urbana: University of Illinois Press, 1985). An excellent examination of this "golden age" in Indiana's history can be found in John Bartlow Martin's *Indiana: An Interpretation* (New York: Alfred A. Knopf, 1947). Also useful for the actions of the Indiana legislature during this period is Justin E. Walsh's *The Centennial History of the Indiana General Assembly, 1816–1978* (Indianapolis: The Select Committee on the Centennial History of the Indiana General Assembly, in cooperation with the Indiana Historical Bureau, 1987).

For this study, Richard John Del Vecchio's "Indiana Politics during the Progressive Era, 1912–1916" (Ph.D. diss., University of Notre Dame, 1973), was particularly helpful, especially his view of reform constituting an integral part of the Hoosier State for many years before the advent of Theodore Roosevelt and the muckrakers.

Although now somewhat outdated, Eldon Cobb Evans's *A History of the Australian Ballot System in the United States* (Chicago: The University of Chicago Press, 1917) offered useful information on the structure of this electoral reform. For a more contemporary account, see L. E. Fredman's *The Australian Ballot: The Story of an American Reform* (East Lansing: Michigan State University Press, 1968). Also useful for this study was Jerrold G. Rusk's "The Effect of the Australian Ballot Reform on Split Ticket Voting: 1876–1908," *American Political Science Review* 64 (December 1970): 1220–38. For Indiana's experience with the Australian ballot system, see Robert LaFollette's "The Adoption of the Australian Ballot in Indiana," *Indiana Magazine of History* 24 (June 1928): 105–20.

The voting methods used by the state before and after the Australian ballot are highlighted in two works: Anna Marie Sander's "A Review of the Election Laws in the State of Indiana from 1787 to 1890" (M.A. thesis, Butler University, 1933), and Charlotte Ethel Bruce's "A Review of Indiana Election Laws, 1889–1935" (M.A. thesis, Butler University, 1935). For an entertaining look at electoral fraud in the state near the turn of the century, Simeon Coy's *The Great Conspiracy: A Complete History of the Famous Tally-Sheet Cases* (Indianapolis: n.p., 1889) ranks with William L. Riordan, comp., *Plunkitt of Tammany Hall: A Series of Very Plain Talks on Very Practical Politics, Delivered by Ex-Senator George Washington Plunkitt, the Tammany Philosopher, from His Rostrum–The New York County Court House Bootblack Stand* (New York: E. P. Dutton, 1963) as a manual for practical politics. On the other side of the coin, the case for reform is eloquently made in William P. Fishback's *A Plea for Honest Elections: An Address Delivered to the Students of the Indiana State University, May, 1886* (Indianapolis: A. R. Baker, Printer, 1886). The Democratic party's efforts at reform are covered exhaustively in David Sarasohn's *The Party of Reform: Democrats in the Progressive Era* (Jackson: University Press of Mississippi, 1989).

The Indianapolis City Charter

Along with Dunn's inside view as offered in Chapter 27, "The City Charter," in *Greater Indianapolis: The History, the Industries, the Institutions, and the People of a City of Homes*, 2 vols. (Chicago: The Lewis Publishing Co., 1910), a useful resource for the city's 1891 charter can be found in Charles Latham, Jr.'s *William Fortune (1863–1942): A Hoosier Biography* (Indianapolis: Guild Press of Indiana, 1994), and the "Government" and "City Charters" entries in David J. Bodenhamer and Robert G. Barrows, eds., *The Encyclopedia of Indianapolis* (Bloomington and Indianapolis: Indiana University Press, 1994).

For details on Indianapolis in the late nineteenth century, see John Bartlow Martin's *Indiana: An Interpretation* (New York: Alfred A. Knopf, 1947) and Hester Anne Hale's *Indianapolis: The First Century* (Indianapolis: Marion County/Indianapolis Historical Society, 1987). A national perspective on the movement for municipal governmental reforms is provided by Samuel P. Hays's *The Response to Industrialism, 1885–1914* (Chicago and London: The University of Chicago Press, 1957) and his article "The Politics of Reform in Municipal Government in the Progressive Era," *Pacific Northwest Quarterly* 55 (October 1964): 157–69. Also helpful for this study was Robert H. Wiebe's exploration of the new urban-industrial order in *The Search for Order, 1877–1920* (New York: Hill and Wang, 1967); Martin J. Schiesl's *The Politics of Efficiency: Municipal Administration and Reform in America, 1880–1920* (Berkeley: University of California Press, 1977); and Ernest S. Griffith's *A History of American City Government: The Conspicuous Failure, 1870–1900* (New York: Praeger Publishers, 1974).

Dunn, Governor Thomas Marshall, and the Indiana Constitution

The only biography of Thomas Marshall is Charles M. Thomas's *Thomas Riley Marshall: Hoosier Statesman* (Oxford, Ohio: Mississippi Valley Press, 1939), which benefited from the support of Marshall's secretary, Mark Thistlethwaite. Although entertaining reading, Marshall's memoir *Recollections of Thomas R. Marshall, Vice President and Hoosier Philosopher: A Hoosier Salad* (Indianapolis: Bobbs-Merrill Co., 1925) offers a limited picture of the Hoosier politician's life. More thorough treatments of Marshall's political career are given in Keith S. Montgomery's "Thomas R. Marshall's Victory in the Election of 1908," *Indiana Magazine of History* 53 (June 1957): 147–66, and Rollo E. Mosher's "Tom Marshall's Term as Governor" (M.A. thesis, Indiana University, 1932). Marshall's papers in the Indiana State Archives and Indiana State Library give detailed accounts of his attitudes about the new Indiana constitution fashioned by Dunn.

Dunn's role in the new Indiana constitution is highlighted in Chapter 13, "An Era of Reform," in the second volume of his *Indiana and Indianans: A History of Aboriginal and Territorial Indiana and the Century of Statehood*, 5 vols. (Chicago and New York: The American Historical Society, 1919). Dunn's arguments for the new constitution and a detailed description of its differences with the 1851 Indiana Constitution can be found in Dunn's *The Proposed Constitution of Indiana* (Indianapolis: Sentinel Printing Co., 1911). A spirited rebuke to Dunn's plan is offered by Christopher Coleman's article "The Development of State Constitutions," *Indiana Magazine of History* 7 (June 1911): 41–51.

The best treatments of the national movement during the Progressive Era to limit the suffrage rights of certain groups can be found in William J. Crotty's *Political Reform and the American Experiment* (New York: Thomas Y. Crowell Co., 1977) and Frances Fox Piven and Richard A. Cloward's *Why Americans Don't Vote* (New York: Pantheon Books, 1989). The latter gives an excellent review of the procedural methods used by reformers to limit voting rights. The suffrage restrictions aimed at immigrants are also explored in Roger Daniels's *Coming to America: A History of Immigration and Ethnicity in American Life* (New York: Harper-Collins, 1990), and John Higham's classic work *Strangers in the Land: Patterns of American Nativism, 1860–1925* (New York: Rutgers University Press, 1955).

For a review of the attempt to revise Indiana's 1851 Constitution, the most extensive examination is in Charles Kettleborough's *Constitution Making in Indiana: A Source Book of Constitutional Documents with Historical Introduction and Critical Notes*, 3 vols. (Indianapolis: Indiana Historical Commission, 1916, 1930). Those consulting this work should be warned that in several instances the documentary material was not transcribed accurately. This is particularly true in the *Ellingham* v. *Dye* (178 Ind. 336–443 [1912]) decision. Later methods at revising the Indiana constitution are examined in John A. Bremer's *Constitution Making in Indiana: A Source Book of Constitutional Documents with Historical Introduction and Critical Notes* (Indianapolis: Indiana Historical Bureau, 1978). The procedures utilized over the years to amend constitutions is covered in Robert Luce's *Legislative Principles: The History and Theory of Lawmaking by Representative Government* (Boston and New York: Houghton Mifflin, 1930) and Albert Lee Sturm's *Methods of State Constitutional Reform* (Ann Arbor: University of Michigan Press, 1954).

Dunn and the Miami Indian Language

The Indiana State Library has the bulk of Dunn's papers concerning his work on the Miami Indian language, including correspondence, reports to the Bureau of American Ethnology, and the cards upon which Dunn compiled his Miami dictionary. As well as detailing the items in this collection, Caroline Dunn's *Jacob Piatt Dunn: His Miami Language Studies and Indian Manuscript Collection, Prehistory Research Series*, vol. 1, no. 2 (Indianapolis: Indiana Historical Society, 1937) provides details on her father's work in this field. Stewart Rafert's exhaustive study, *The Miami Indians of Indiana: A Persistent People,*

1654–1994 (Indianapolis: Indiana Historical Society, 1996) also proved to be extremely helpful for the Miami's plight and Dunn's role in helping to preserve the tribe's language.

Dunn's often passionate defense for keeping alive the Miami language shines through in such books and articles as *True Indian Stories* (Indianapolis: Sentinel Printing Co., 1909); "Misunderstood Mythology," *Americana* (April 1923): 180–85; and "A Language Clue to Indian Origins," *The Red Man* (March-April 1917): 196–200.

Index

Designer: Dean Johnson Design, Inc., Indianapolis, Indiana
Typeface: New Century Schoolbook
Typographer: Douglas & Gayle Limited, Indianapolis, Indiana
Paper: 70-pound Cougar Opaque Natural
Printer: BookCrafters, Chelsea, Michigan